CONGRATULATIONS ON YOUR GRADUATION!

_____

_____

_____

Jim and Jane Pratt set out to write a 'how-to-succeed at life' handbook for their kids who were about to graduate from high school. They did more than that – they in fact wrote an owner's manual – important for every person who wants a shot at succeeding in life.

—*Dr. David Twist, B.Sc., M.D., FRCPC, Chief of Anaesthesiology,*
Surrey Memorial Hospital, and Clinical Instructor, University of British Columbia

Our children have so many distractions and many live in a culture where values have become warped. *Turtle on a Fence Post* is a must-read for young people about to embark on their independent lives. Over the ensuing years, they will learn many life lessons, but *Turtle*'s 365 life lessons will accelerate that learning dramatically, save them time and, in some cases, embarrassment. Brilliant in its simplicity and powerful in its content – this is a sure bet.

—*John Rothwell, President, Canaccord Wealth Management*

Call it the student's compass to the galaxy. In today's fast-changing world, *Turtle on a Fence Post* provides valuable lessons to navigate everything from academics to careers to social events to relationships. Whether uplifting affirmations or etiquette tips, the authors point you in the right direction. The Pratts have set high standards… to see youth strive to fulfill their own individual goals.

—*Brent Jang, Globe and Mail reporter, a National Newspaper Award winner,*
former editor-in-chief of U of Alberta's The Gateway

Mr. and Mrs. Pratt have done such a fine job in offering perhaps the best gift to their children. *Turtle on a Fence Post* is one of the best self-help books I have ever read due to its simplicity yet extreme practicality based on the authors' best experiences and observations in life as accomplished business persons and parents.

I will certainly recommend it to my two young children as they are growing up, and will share it with my students and colleagues.

—*Dr. Jacqueline Shan, Ph.D., D.Sc., ICD.D, Co-founder and*
Chief Scientific Officer, Afexa Life Sciences Inc., and co-inventor of COLD-FX™

This book belongs on the bookshelf of every high school graduate, and anyone who wants a jumpstart on success – young or old. It's a quick read, but don't let that fool you – it's packed full of hints and lessons that will help any reader achieve their goals.

—*Dr. Terry Zachary, inventor of the Handmaster Plus™, former touring golf professional*
and author of The Power of Golf

What an insightful daily manual for living a well-rounded and healthy life! I sure wish I had had this 'manual' when I left home. I can't wait to give a copy to my daughter when she's old enough!

—Brian Scudamore, Founder and CEO of 1-800-GOT-JUNK?, 2007 International Franchise Association Entrepreneur of the Year, Fortune Small Business Best Boss Award winner and a five-time Ernst & Young's Entrepreneur of the Year finalist

A helpful and informative guide that inspires and guides the graduate as he/she embarks on the rest of life's journey. *Turtle on a Fence Post* would be beneficial (maybe essential) to any high school graduate.

—Don Horwood, Retired University Basketball Coach, three time CIS National Champion, 15 national tournament appearances, three-time CIS coach of the year

Jim and Jane have not only focused on issues that high school graduates deal with, they have also courageously addressed the struggles which everyone faces regardless of age – vocations, relationships, entertainment, sexuality, ethics, morality, and also spirituality. Well done, Jim and Jane!

—Pastor Paul Fast and Betty Fast, his beloved wife of 50 years

Competing internationally as a part of Team Canada Beach Volleyball for 5 years, I have dealt with the excitement and also the many pressures and disappointments that befall a professional athlete. Often, a poignant thought, poem or 'kick in the butt' is all that is necessary to 'get back on the horse' after a week or month of letdowns. This book provides the reader with just that.

For a daily dose of quality life lessons provided from a collection of highly successful individuals who have 'been there', I recommend this book. It's a great guide – a unique dynamic of spiritual and social lessons.

—Rich Van Huizen, Canadian National Beach Volleyball Team member, professional beach volleyball player on FIVB tour from 2003 to present

A succinct, much-needed book that every young person should read. *Turtle on a Fence Post* is a concise, readable, how-to-live guide that high school graduates can use in everyday life, every day of the year, to make a successful transition to a meaningful adult life.

—Steve Campbell, author, Third & Long: Men's Playbook for Solving Marital/Relationship Troubles and Building a Winning Team

TURTLE ON A FENCE POST

JIM AND JANE PRATT

PUBLISHING HOUSE

Author photos by jmbphotography.ca

For information and bulk orders, please go to
www.turtleonafencepost.ca

PUBLISHING HOUSE

151 HOWE STREET, VICTORIA BC CANADA V8V 4K5

info@agiopublishing.com or go to
www.agiopublishing.com

ISBN 978-1-897435-31-1 (clothbound with jacket)
10 9 8 7 6 5 4 3 2 1b

Printed on acid-free paper.

This book is dedicated to our children Elizabeth, David and Michael.
"We are truly blessed to have you as our children.
The world is a better place because you are in it."

Dear Kids,

Our time with you as children is over. You are about to embark on that great adventure called adulthood.

With the benefit of hindsight, we can say with certainty that you, like us, will face many challenges. Along with the challenges, there will be triumphs. It is a cliché, but life is like a roller coaster. Sometimes these ups and downs happen very fast, and we are reassured by the knowledge that you have a strong foundation and will be able to cope with them.

We have watched you grow from toddlers – whose only job was to eat, sleep, and make Mommy and Daddy smile – to teenagers trying to figure out who you are. Every day with you has been a joy (some more than others). Every day we tried to forge a foundation that would help you become the best people you could possibly be. Every day brought a new lesson, either for you or for us.

As you now prepare to leave the comforts and security of home, we offer you something tangible to take on your journey. It is our book of life lessons. These are the pearls we have collected over the years the hard way – through experience. Our sincere hope is that this collection will help you with the ups, downs and curves of adulthood.

Just like in life, we encourage you to take these lessons one day at a time. Read one lesson each day. Learn from all of them.

Your adventure is about to begin. Read well, live well, and always try to make the choices that are right for you and those you love.

With love,
Mom & Dad

THANK YOU AND ACKNOWLEDGEMENTS

It is impossible to thank everyone who provided us with life lessons over the years. And so we won't even try. However we can readily acknowledge who our greatest teachers were – they were our parents: Kay Haluschak, Frank Haluschak, Bev Pratt and Jim Pratt. We are the people we are today because of your guidance and your influence. Thank you.

We'd like to thank some people who were a big help in pulling this book together: Brent Jang and Steve Campbell for their feedback and encouragement, Jordan Maddox, Jane Keyes for help in editing, and George Lin for his help with graphics and layout. Also a big thank you goes to Marsha and Bruce Batchelor at Agio Publishing House for their guidance, patient hand-holding and creativity.

We've tried to ensure that we have acknowledged all of the authors of the various quotes and stories found in the book. It is not our intention to avoid giving anyone their proper due and we apologize in advance if you've not been given proper credit. If we have missed you, please let us know and we'll make the corrections in future editions.

MONDAY Motivational

TUESDAY Career Advancement

WEDNESDAY Career Advancement

THURSDAY General Life Lessons

FRIDAY General Life Lessons

SATURDAY Socializing

SUNDAY Spiritual

INTRODUCTION

This book includes many lessons we consider vital to helping graduates make it in the real world. High school and university textbooks provide the book smarts; we hope this will help with the "life smarts."

The idea for this book began as our oldest approached her high school graduation. We asked ourselves: as parents, have we done everything possible to help our daughter make it in the "real world"? Has she heard the messages we've tried to convey over the years? We knew that school had taught her the three Rs, but had she also learned our life lessons while growing up? Now, with two other soon-to-graduate teenagers, we decided we wanted to put together a "life after high school" reference book – sort of a guide to help our children navigate the complicated world they and their friends will face after graduation.

It's one of the ironic twists of raising children that the effort expended by parents to pass on the pearls of wisdom that will help their children become successful adults occurs at a time when those young ears are not very receptive to Mom and Dad telling them… well, anything. Yes, it's the teenage years. There is the story of a high school principal who jokingly encourages her students to drop out of school when they are fifteen so that they can "go out and get a job now, while [they] know everything." And we are reminded of Mark Twain, who commented that at sixteen years old he was embarrassed by how little his father knew, but was astounded by how much his father had learned by the time Mark had turned twenty!

In short, we wanted to give our kids something they could take away with them to refer to when they needed guidance. And, because in our view it is important to learn something new every day, we divided the book into 365 days of lessons. Each day's lesson was kept short so that it could be read quickly over breakfast or during a break. We applied a theme to each day of the week. Monday's theme happens to be motivational, because Mondays can be tough to face. Tuesday and Wednesday offer helpful hints for advancing careers. Thursday and Friday deal with general life lessons. Saturday offers help with the social aspects of life, while Sunday focuses on spiritual guidance taken from a cross-section of different religions and teachers.

Many of the anecdotes or quotes included in this book will no doubt seem familiar. Some are truisms and some are stories that have been circulating around cyberspace for years. We've included them because they help to impart and reinforce messages we believe are important. In cases where a source is unknown, we have taken the liberty of inserting 'Grandpa Frank' into the story. Grandpa Frank was a teacher and school principal who grew up on a farm on the Canadian Prairies during the Depression years. More importantly, he was Jane's father. He passed away when she was 15 years old, not long before Jane herself graduated from high school.

We hope this book will help thousands of young graduates on their paths to success.

Jane and Jim Pratt
(aka Mom and Dad)

TURTLE ON A FENCE POST

1 A Journey Of 1,000 Miles Begins With A Single Step

— Lao Tzu, c. 604 BC

When faced with a job or task that at the outset seems daunting, the best thing to do is… just get started.

You cannot finish something if you do not start it. Even if your first step seems like an insignificant one, get going; that first step will put you one step closer to finishing.

2 Listen and silent contain the same letters

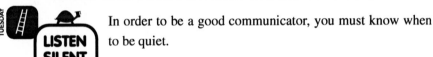

In order to be a good communicator, you must know when to be quiet.

The ability to communicate effectively is an important life skill. One key to becoming more effective is to understand that being a good communicator begins with being a good listener – not with being a good talker. Make sure you understand what the other person is saying before you respond. Good communication begins *and continues* with good listening. This means you should be quiet more than you are verbal during conversations.

3 Life can only be understood backwards; but it must be lived forwards

— Soren (1813–1855)

It makes good sense to try to learn from the people around you who are more experienced. In many cases, this means listening to what your elders have to say. Chances are they have already lived through (or observed) what you are now experiencing. Ask them for advice and pay attention to it.

SUCCESS SIMPLY MEANS TO FOLLOW THROUGH

The Roman author Syrus (first century BC) said: "Many receive advice, only the wise profit from it." You can profit from somebody else's knowledge today.

4 Passion drives perfection

THURSDAY

— *Rick Warren (b. 1954)*

Only if you are passionate about something, will you excel at it.

If you hope to do something extremely well, make sure you develop a passion for it. The more passionate you are about something – whether it's getting on the Dean's list, making a varsity sports team, or having a healthy relationship with your family – the easier it will be to achieve and the more success you'll ultimately enjoy.

5 The measure of a man is what he would do if he knew he would never be found out

FRIDAY

— *Thomas Macaulay (1800–1859)*

There are many temptations in life.

There is the temptation to take shortcuts at school, such as copying someone's homework; there is the temptation to drive through a red light at two o'clock in the morning when no one is around to see; there is sexual temptation. Everyone faces temptation in their life. The challenge is to not give in, even if you know there is a good chance you won't be caught.

Make sure that, when you decide to measure yourself, you'll like the result.

SATURDAY

6 Some table manners to remember when dining in public

Posture: Always sit up straight and do not lean backward or forward in your chair. When eating, avoid bringing your face toward the plate; rather, bring the fork or spoon up to you. And remember that your elbows should never touch the table (although it is okay for your hands to do so).

Passing things: If someone asks for something to be passed, reach for it only if you are the person closest to that item. If you are, pick it up and place it directly next to your neighbor. Avoid passing it hand-to-hand unless your neighbor makes a grab for it. You should not help yourself to the item until the original requester has finished with it. When that person is done, you can ask for the item to be passed back to you. If someone asks you to pass only the salt, pass both the salt and pepper together. And you should not use the salt (or pepper) until after the original requester has had a chance to use it. Finally, with respect to salt and pepper, you should never season your food until after you have tasted it – it is an insult to the chef to add flavor before tasting.

Mouth mishaps: If you inadvertently burp or hiccup, excuse yourself quietly and put your napkin to your lips.

Napkin etiquette: Your napkin should be used to "dab" your mouth. Avoid wiping your mouth or face vigorously. At the end of the meal, your napkin should not be crumpled or twisted (this conveys either untidiness or nervousness), nor should it be folded up (because it may give the impression that you think your host might be able to reuse it without washing it). Simply place the napkin to the side of your plate. The napkin should not be left on the seat of your chair when you leave. There is a European superstition that the diner who leaves his or her napkin on the chair will never sit at that table again.

Dealing with spills: Accidents happen. So, if you spill something, don't make a big deal about it. Quietly apologize and make an effort to ensure that nothing will drip onto the people sitting next to you. It is acceptable to use your napkin to stem the flow of any liquid. If something does get onto someone else's clothes, don't attempt to clean it off. Bring it to their attention, apologize, and let them clean it up. You should also offer to pay the dry-cleaning bill.

7 The Confederate Soldier

SUNDAY

I asked God for strength, that I might achieve;
I was made weak that I might obey.
I asked for health that I might do greater things;
I was given infirmity that I might do better things.
I asked for riches that I might be happy;
I was given poverty that I might be wise.

I asked for power that I might have the praise of men;
I was given weakness that I might feel the need of God.

I asked for all things that I might enjoy life;
I was given life that I might enjoy all things.

I received nothing that I asked for, but all I had hoped for.
My prayer was answered, I am most richly blessed.

> — *Written by an unknown Confederate soldier.*

8 The value of training

MONDAY

The duration of an athletic contest is only a few minutes, while the training for it may take weeks of arduous work and continuous exercise of self-effort. The real value of sport is not the actual game played in the limelight of applause, but the hours of dogged determination and self-discipline carried out alone, imposed and supervised by an exacting conscience. The applause soon dies away, the prize is left behind, but the character you build up is yours forever.

> —*Author Unknown*

This is what sports (or music, or dance, etc.) is about. It is not about million-dollar salaries or fan adulation; it is about character-building.

Very few people make a living from professional sports, music or art. However, you can be sure that every successful person – no matter what their field – has had to train hard for something in the past, and has successfully applied those lessons to other areas of their life.

9 Be very careful what you write in an email or post on a website

Remember that emails are a permanent written record and can be sent at the push of a button to hundreds of people. Before sending anything by email, visualize whatever you write as being posted on the company or school bulletin board. If you wouldn't want it to be seen there, don't write it in an email.

Do not surf the web for non-business-related topics while at work. There are two reasons for this: first, during business hours your time should be dedicated to your employer, who pays your salary and therefore deserves your undivided attention; second, computers and/or networks retain a history of sites visited. You may be embarrassed if your employer sees some of the personal sites you visit.

10 There is no I in TEAM, but there is an M and an E

TEAM
I ME

At first glance, this sentence may seem to contain a contradiction. But it doesn't.

The first part accurately describes that a successful team should not have a focus on any one individual. For every superstar that won a championship, there was a strong supporting cast. Michael Jordan had Scottie Pippen; Wayne Gretzky had Mark Messier; Terry Bradshaw had Franco Harris.

Notwithstanding the above, there is a place for ME in a successful team. The ME mindset means that every individual has to be accountable to the team. In fact, without the ME mindset, a team cannot be successful. Each person must understand that they have a certain role and a responsibility to the team. They must understand that "I have a job to do and it is up to ME to do it right. If I don't, then I will let the team down."

11 A friend must not be injured, even in jest

THURSDAY O₂

— Publilius Syrus (1st Century B.C.)

Substitute the words "loved one" for "friend" to get a broader lesson from this quote.

Familiarity can lead us to take our friends and loved ones for granted. Sometimes it can cause us to forget they have feelings that can be hurt. Consider how polite or how careful you are when you speak to people you don't know well. Most of us would never make a derogatory joke about someone's hairstyle or choice of clothes if we had just met them. So, don't make a potentially hurtful joke about a loved one just because you are comfortable with that individual. Not only could your comment hurt that person, you could be judged poorly by others who might be within earshot.

Now, good-natured ribbing is a part of friendship; however, be careful not to cross the line from "ribbing" to "rubbing" the wrong way. Your friendship will dictate where this line is, but to be safe it is best not to do it at all – then you won't have to worry about crossing any line.

12 Anger is one letter away from danger

Getting angry is perfectly natural when you have been wronged in some way. Throughout life, it is likely that not a day will go by during which you won't be completely justified in getting angry about one thing or another.

However, be very careful in your responses. Just as in sports, it is the retaliation that often draws the penalty. Don't let your responses get you into trouble.

13 Learn how to cook at least one good recipe

SATURDAY

If you like to cook, great. But even if you don't, learn to cook at least one good recipe that you can make in short order. Among other things, an ability to cook shows people a couple of things about you: that you like to provide enjoyment for people (because everybody likes to eat), and that you have diverse talents. A spin-off benefit of your culinary skills is that you will probably get invited out to dinner more often because people will feel compelled to reciprocate!

14 The most perfect among men is he who loves his neighbor without thinking about whether the person is good or bad

SUNDAY

— Muhammad (570 – 632)

It is easy to accept someone if you have something in common with them or if they are nice to you. The more difficult thing is to embrace them when they are different from you or if they treat you badly. Nevertheless, try to accept people regardless of how you feel about them. You will be a better person for it.

15 Create your own future... or fall into somebody else's

MONDAY

— Ian Angell (b. 1947)

It is important to fully utilize your talents and skills in order to make the best possible life for yourself and your family. Not working to improve yourself is a waste.

It will be a rare occurrence that another person will do something to make your life better for you without an ulterior motive. If you want your life to be better, you will have to do something about it yourself.

If you fail to use your skills to pursue opportunities (careers, relationships, education, etc.), your life will be determined by others.

16 Hints for public speaking

Toastmaster's International (www.toastmasters.org), an organization dedicated to the improvement of public speaking, has many helpful hints to keep in mind when giving a speech or presentation. Four important ones are as follows:

1. **"Remove the ing."** Avoid distracting mannerisms such as rocking, swaying, gripping, tapping, licking your lips, playing with coins, adjusting, etc.

2. **"Talk to me."** Be natural, spontaneous and conversational. The single most important rule for helping you to look relaxed and comfortable is to be yourself. Think of your speech as an "enlarged conversation" rather than a "dramatic performance." Just remember that you are speaking to a larger audience and so you will need to exaggerate what you would normally do in a conversation: make your gestures a little bit bigger, open your mouth a little bit wider, and exaggerate your facial expressions somewhat.

3. **"Mirror, mirror, on the wall."** Let your body mirror your feelings. Dale Carnegie (1888–1955) said, "A speaker who is interested will usually be interesting." The audience needs to know how you feel about your subject, and thus it is important that your body language convey your feelings and attitudes.

4. **"Go with the flow."** You will look confident if you are thoroughly prepared. Nothing influences a speaker's attitude more than the knowledge that he or she is well prepared. This knowledge will translate into self-confidence, a key ingredient in effective public speaking. When you are prepared, you will be less tense because you

are not worried about what to say next. Accordingly, it is important to practice and rehearse your speech while avoiding actual memorization. The conscious effort required to recall the speech verbatim will make you seem nervous and tense. If you know the material well enough, you will only need a flow of ideas to help guide you through your presentation. You can use slides or visual aids to help you with this. On each slide, have a couple of words that serve as a prompt to aid you in remembering what you wanted to say, and also to provide some structure to your presentation.

17 The Janitor

Near the end of the term in the MBA Leadership Course, the professor would often give the class a surprise quiz. The quiz was usually pretty easy, and most students would zip through all the questions – until the last one. It would be: "What is the first name of the man who cleans the business school?"

Most students would think it was a joke. After all, they were MBA students about to graduate with a degree that would help them command very high salaries in the business world. Most didn't "have time" for the janitor. He was an old man, way past his prime, with a stooped back and arthritic hands from years of hard work, and he had a thick Scottish accent. Nobody ever talked to him.

Many students would hand in the quiz, leaving that last question blank and thinking it wouldn't count for anything. Invariably, somebody would eventually ask if the last question counted toward the final grade. "Absolutely," the prof would say. "In your careers as business leaders, you will meet many people. Remember that all are significant to your company's success. Every employee deserves your attention, even if all you do is smile and say 'hello.'"

— *Author Unknown*

Bright students never forget this lesson.

(By the way, his name was Jimmy.)

...ANOTHER IS GIVEN IN ITS PLACE

18 Experience is not what happens to you. It is what you do with what happens to you

THURSDAY

— Aldous Huxley (1894 – 1963)

You *can* learn something new everyday.

Understand that you have the chance to learn from every experience, good or otherwise. Take advantage of that opportunity to learn something so that you better yourself – physically, financially and emotionally. Cultivate a willingness to try new things and combine this with an attitude that you want to learn from those experiences. The result will be that you will grow and improve as a person.

19 Body Reading

The ability to read body language is a helpful skill to develop, and one that will improve over time as you interact with more and more people in different situations. Being able to interpret body language offers a chance to garner valuable information that is often not apparent from what people are actually verbalizing.

Some of the more obvious body language messages include the following: crossed arms, meaning "I am not receptive"; a turned back, which means "you or what you say are not important to me"; and droopy eyes, which say "I am bored." More subtle ones include eyes looking up to the left, or a "V" shape between the eyebrows; these often accompany lying. Constricted pupils can indicate interest or emotion in a subject. Similarly, flushed cheeks can point to interest in the topic – or that the listener is hiding something.

One important thing to remember about body language is that gestures mean different things in different parts of the world. Below are a few accepted North American gestures or body movements that, when traveling in the various countries or regions listed below, can actually be construed as insults.

In Brazil, Australia, Spain and the Middle East: the circular "OK" sign and the "thumbs up" sign;

In Great Britain: the "V" for victory sign or the "peace" sign with the back of your fingers facing the other person; and

In Islamic countries: showing the soles of your feet (such as when sitting down).

20 Toasts (drinking, not the bread kind)

SATURDAY

There are as many different toasts in the world as there are countries. Some examples:

- **United Kingdom**: Cheers!
- **Canada:** Cheemo!
- **China:** Wen Lie!
- **France:** A votre sante!
- **Germany:** Prosit!
- **Greece:** Yasas!
- **Hebrew:** L'Chayim!
- **Hungary:** Ege'sze'ge're!
- **Ireland:** Slainte!
- **Italy:** Alla Salute!
- **Japan:** Kanpai!
- **Poland:** Na Zdrowie!
- **Russia:** Za vashe zdorovye!
- **Spain:** Salud!
- **Sweden:** Skal!

It is helpful to know one or two unique toasts. Here are some to consider:

To health and prosperity: May you live as long as you like, and have all you like as long as you live.

To friendship: Old wood to burn,

Old books to read,

Old wine to drink,

Old friends to trust.

To better times: A speedy calm to the storms of life.

To loved ones: May the warmth of our affections survive the frosts of age.

21 Much of what you need to know in life can be learned from the story of Noah's Ark

SUNDAY

1. Don't miss the boat.
2. Remember that we are all in the same boat.
3. Plan ahead. It wasn't raining when Noah started building the Ark.
4. Stay fit. No matter how old you are, someone may ask you to do something really important.
5. Don't listen to critics. Just get on with the job that needs to be done.
6. Build your future on high ground.
7. For safety's sake, travel in pairs.
8. Speed isn't always an advantage. The snails were on board with the cheetahs.
9. When you are stressed, float awhile.
10. No matter the storm, when you are with God there's always a rainbow waiting.

— *Author Unknown*

22 Grandpa Frank used to tell the story of Bill the carpenter

MONDAY

Bill had been a carpenter for forty years and was ready to retire. He told his boss that he wanted to retire so he could spend more time with his wife and enjoy his grandchildren. His boss was disappointed because Bill had been an excellent employee and a very good worker. Nevertheless, he understood Bill's position, and asked Bill if he would build one final house as a personal favor. Bill agreed, but he knew his heart would not be in it; he had lost his enthusiasm for the job. Not surprisingly, his workmanship ended up being shoddy. It was an unfortunate way to end a very good career.

When Bill had finished building the house, his boss came to do the final inspection. Even before he started the inspection, he handed the front door key to Bill, saying, "Bill, this is your house, my gift to you for your years of excellent work and faithful service." Bill was shocked and surprised, but soon felt ashamed. He thought to himself that had he known he was building his own house, he would have done it differently. Now he would be living in a house he had built poorly.

— *Author Unknown*

The lesson here is that many people do the same thing: they live their lives not trying to do their best. Later in life, they are disappointed when they reflect on their life and find they are living in a house that was not built well. Had they realized earlier what they were doing, they would have done things differently.

Think of yourself as Bill. Think about your life as a house. Each day you are adding to your life by hammering in a nail, cutting some wood and putting up the walls.

23 Business networking

Before you attend a business-related event, ask yourself what you'd like to get out of it on both a professional and personal level. Go in with a goal in mind regardless of how small or trivial it may be. The goal might be to meet a client that you cannot seem to connect with by telephone, or it might be to display your interaction skills to your

...THAN HE WHO THINKS HIMSELF SO

boss, or it might be simply to market yourself as a potential employee. Most business events can lead to personal benefits as well. Take every opportunity to develop and expand your network.

24 Getting to talk to the boss

There will be times when you'll need to talk to senior people in your organization or at your school – people such as the company president or the dean of the faculty. Most of these people will have an assistant or secretary to serve as a "gatekeeper" to screen their calls or set up meetings. It is important to develop a friendly relationship with these gatekeepers beforehand so as to predispose them to granting your request. Find out who those people are, get to know them, and treat them with respect; in short, always behave as if you are speaking directly to your employer.

25 There are three ways to help fight jet lag

1. Drink lots of fluids, preferably water (and no alcohol);
2. Eat lightly the day before traveling; and
3. Upon arrival, fall immediately into the local rhythm of meals and sleep.

26 Stressed spelled backwards is desserts

Stress is a fact of life. Get used to dealing with it, because you will not be able to avoid it.

There are many ways to deal with stress, some more acceptable than others. Exercise is good – alcohol and drugs are not. Some people like to talk through their problems. Other people have hobbies to distract themselves.

Make sure, when you do get stressed, that you take the time to do something to help relieve the tension. Do something nice for yourself.

27 How to work a revolving door

SATURDAY

When you approach a revolving door with a colleague or friend, it is polite to go through the revolving door first so that you are the one pushing the door – but always say "allow me" prior to going before them.

28 A rich person is not the one who has the most, but the one who needs the least

SUNDAY

— *Dalai Lama (b. 1935)*

If you are happy with your life right here and now – your health, your job, your family – you are rich no matter how much money you have in the bank. If having money, cars, houses or expensive toys is required to make you feel "rich," then the sad reality is that you will never achieve that feeling. Someone – your neighbor, your cousin, the mail-room guy – will have more, thereby making you feel poorer.

It is important to learn what is really important in life – and to understand that the fewer material things you need, the richer you are.

Proverbs 21:17 says, "He who loves pleasure will become a poor man." Don't become poor.

29 The Peasant and the Boulder

MONDAY

In ancient times, a king had a big boulder placed on a roadway. He hid and waited to see if anyone would remove the huge rock. Some of the king's wealthiest merchants and courtiers came by and simply walked around it. Many loudly blamed the king for not keeping the roads clear, but nobody did anything about moving it out of the way.

Then a peasant came by pulling a hand cart filled with heavy hides. When he came up to the boulder, he dropped the cart and began trying to move it to the side of the road. After much pushing and straining, he finally succeeded. As the peasant went to pick up the cart to be on his way, he noticed a purse lying in the pothole where the boulder had been. Opening the purse, he found that it contained a number of gold coins and a note. The note, written by the king, said that the gold was to be kept by the person who took the initiative to remove the obstacle.

— Author Unknown

The experience taught the peasant something that most people never learn: every obstacle presents an opportunity to improve your condition.

30 The Dress Code

TUESDAY

If you are ever in doubt about the dress code at work, take your cues from the senior people running the company. Look to what they wear and make the effort to dress as well as, or better than, they do. Your dress will reflect your opinion of the company. Well dressed = high opinion. Poorly dressed = low opinion. Make sure you reflect favorably.

31 To be successful in your career, possibly the most important skill you will need to possess is dependability

WEDNESDAY

You possess a unique set of talents and abilities that you bring to your school, team, family or workplace. Some people are blessed with an abundance of skills – good with numbers, high intelligence, strong negotiating ability. Regardless of what you are blessed with, understand that the one ability most appreciated by an employer is dependability. And, since it is an acquired skill, anyone who wishes to develop dependability can do so simply by making the choice.

If you cannot or will not do what is expected of you, you will not be successful. Be dependable.

32 It's not a mistake until you do it twice

Within reason, never be afraid to try something (unless, of course, that something would cause physical or emotional harm to you or someone else). But don't be afraid to try something new because you are afraid of making a mistake. A mistake doesn't really count as a mistake unless you have made the same one before.

33 To acquire knowledge, one must study; but to acquire wisdom, one must observe

— Marilyn Vos Savant (b. 1946)

There are three ways to become "smart":

1. **Study hard in school**. You've heard the term "book smart" to describe someone who gets good marks in school. It is very important to do well in school. However, books cannot teach you everything you need to know to be a success. That's where the next two items come in.

2. **Experience life.** In order to get a well-rounded education, you need to learn from actually experiencing things as well. And while some will be enjoyable, expect other experiences to be painful.

3. **Observe**. Learn from other people's experiences. If you can watch and learn from others – particularly from recognizing their mistakes – then you can learn a lesson or two without experiencing the pain.

One of Aesop's fables illustrates this last point.

The Lion, the Fox, and the Ass

A Lion, a Fox and an Ass entered into an agreement to assist each other in the hunt for food. Having secured a large booty, on their return from the forest the Lion asked the Ass to allot his due portion to each of the three partners in the treaty. The Ass carefully divided the spoil into three equal shares and modestly requested the two others to make the first choice. The Lion, bursting out into a great rage, devoured the Ass.

...IMAGINATION OVER INTELLIGENCE

Then he requested the Fox to do him the favor to divide up the catch. The Fox accumulated all that they had killed into one large heap and left to himself the smallest possible morsel. The Lion said, "Who has taught you, my very excellent fellow, the art of division? You are perfect to a fraction." The Fox replied, "I learned it from the Ass, by witnessing his fate."

34 Never do anything until the host does it first

Whenever you are invited out to dinner, whether at someone's home or in a restaurant, there will be a host (usually, although not always, it is the person who extended the invitation). In all respects, you should take the lead for any action from your host. The host should always go first – first to toast, first to eat, first to leave the table. He or she should also be the first to sit down, except if you've been asked to do so – which you should do immediately when asked. Whatever the setting, the host is paying for the meal, so it is important he or she be made to feel in charge.

35 Facing Challenges

There will be very challenging times in your life: losing your job, troubles in your marriage, troubles with your teenage kids, a loved one passing away. At these times, people often ask, "God, why are you doing this to me?" During times like these, keep in mind that God is a loving God and He knows what is best for us. Just like any mother or father who wants the best for their children, God does as well – as difficult as it may seem at times.

You will not be alone in your challenges. Everyone has struggles and difficulties. Even Mother Teresa (1910 – 1997), winner of the Nobel Peace Prize and a much-admired person around the world, expressed frustration about her life challenges. She said, "I know God would never give me something that I could not handle... I just wish He wouldn't trust me so much."

During those times when you will feel that life's challenges are just too much, remember that God will only give you what you can handle. Try to make the best of the situation. Don't ask "Why are you doing this to me?" Instead, ask, "What are you trying to teach me?"

The answer to this question may give you a helpful lesson.

36 The Ring

One day King Solomon decided he needed to teach a lesson to his most trusted minister, who had become a bit of a "know-it-all." He said to him, "Benaiah, there is a certain ring I want you to bring to me. I wish to wear it for Sukkot, the Feast of Tabernacles, which gives you six months to find it."

"If it exists anywhere on earth, Your Majesty," replied Benaiah, "I will find it and bring it to you. But what makes the ring so special?"

"It has magic powers," answered the King. "If a happy man looks at it he becomes sad, and if a sad man looks at it he becomes happy." King Solomon knew that no such ring existed, but he wished to put his minister in his place.

Months passed but Benaiah could not find it. Distraught, on the night before Sukkot he took a walk in one of the poorest quarters of Jerusalem. He ended up passing by a very old merchant who was in the process of putting away his wares from an old shabby carpet. "Have you by any chance heard of a magic ring that makes the happy wearer forget his joy and the broken-hearted wearer forget his sorrows?" asked Benaiah.

To his surprise, the old merchant nodded, picked up a plain gold ring from his carpet and engraved something on it. When Benaiah read the words on the ring, his face broke out in a wide smile.

The next night, the entire city was in the square and welcomed in the holiday of Sukkot with great festivity. "Well, my friend," said King

Solomon, "have you found what I sent you after?" All the ministers laughed and King Solomon himself smiled, because they all knew there was no such ring.

To everyone's surprise, Benaiah held up a small gold ring and declared, "Here it is, Your Majesty!" As soon as Solomon read the inscription, the smile vanished from his face. The jeweler had written three Hebrew letters on the gold band, which began the words "Gam zeh ya'avor" meaning "this too shall pass."

At that moment, King Solomon was crestfallen; he realized that all his wisdom, fabulous wealth and tremendous power were but fleeting things, for one day he would be nothing but dust.

> — *Jewish folktale*

You need to be aware that both the good times and the bad times will eventually fade away. Enjoy the good times when they occur and don't dwell on the bad times. Time will erase both.

37 The lady doth protest too much, methinks

> — *spoken by Queen Gertrude in Hamlet (III, ii, 239)*
> *by William Shakespeare (1564–1616)*

In Hamlet, one of the characters, Queen Gertrude, speaks these words to her son, Prince Hamlet, while she is watching a play (yes, a play within a play). She speaks these words after hearing the Queen in the play going "overboard" about her love and loyalty to the King.

What Gertrude does not realize is that Hamlet, her son, has staged this scene in the play to try to trap her and her new husband, King Claudius (Hamlet's stepfather), whom Hamlet suspects of having murdered his father. She does not realize that the Queen in the play who "doth protest too much" is actually herself. The Queen's repetitive pledges of loyalty and love toward her first husband are, of course, false, because she was involved in his killing. The audience, including Queen Gertrude herself, can easily see through this ruse.

The message here is to be cautious of people who are overly vocal about a topic or subject. They are likely either trying to hide something, or they are trying to divert your attention away from something. Be wary.

38 There's no use looking up a dead horse's ass

— Prairie proverb

When something bad happens to you, it is often best to just forget about it rather than dwell on it. The reality is that you can't change what has happened in the past – but you can learn something from it. Put it behind you and move on.

39 Eating Right

The U.S. Department of Agriculture (USDA) has recently revised the food pyramid and reworked its recommendations for daily food intake.

The new pyramid is divided into vertical sections rather than the horizontal ones that were used before. The new pyramid is also color-coded, and each section is sized to represent the ratio of each type of food we should be eating in a day.

In general terms, the changes to the food pyramid are meant to highlight the need for more exercise, fewer calories and wholesome nutrition.

Beginning on the left side of the pyramid is the first section (section 1). This is the largest slice and it represents the grains. The USDA recommends that grains should comprise the largest part of the daily diet, and suggests that at least half of these should be whole grains. Grains include things such as bread, pasta, rice and cereal. Whole grains include brown rice, oatmeal, whole wheat and rye bread.

The next slice to the right (Section 2) represents vegetables. The USDA suggests that an 18-year-old should consume up to three cups of vegetables per day, particularly if he or she is active (defined as exercising for thirty minutes per day).

The next one (Section 3) represents fruits. Fruits add vitamins, minerals and fiber to a diet. A recommended daily serving for an active 18-year-old is two cups of fruit per day.

Section 4 represents fats, oils and sweets. Fats and oils are necessary for healthy bodily function, but should be consumed sparingly. Similarly, sweets should be consumed in moderation, if at all. Many cereals and breads have added sugar, and so it is probably not necessary to eat sweets on a daily basis.

Section 5 represents dairy, including milk, yogurt and cheese, and provides essential proteins and calcium. An active 18-year-old's daily allowance of dairy is three cups.

The section on the far right (6) represents meats, fish, beans and nuts. These supply the body with protein, vitamin-B complex and iron. It is recommended that an 18-year-old consume up to six ounces from this group per day.

The staircase on the left side of the pyramid represents daily exercise.

In summary, an 18-year-old should:
1. Exercise every day; and
2. Consume lots of grains, three cups of vegetables, three cups of dairy, two cups of fruit, a little bit of fats and oils, and six ounces of protein (meat, fish, beans or nuts) each day.

40 Drinking and Driving

Under no circumstances – *ever* – should you drink and drive. By "drink," we mean alcohol in quantities that will impair your judgment. Make sure you know your limit, and stay well below it if you have to drive.

Equally important is not to get in a car with anyone who has been drinking alcohol. Ever. You don't know their limit and you don't know whether their judgment is impaired. If there is any doubt about you or your friend's ability to drive, call another friend or a family member for a ride, no matter what time of day or night it is. A friend or loved one would rather be awakened from a deep sleep to drive you home than to go identify you at the morgue.

The following poem has been around for a while now and sends a powerful message.

Went to a Party, Mom

I went to a party,
　　And remembered what you said.
　　You told me not to drink, Mom
　　So I had a Sprite instead.
I felt proud of myself,
　　The way you said I would,
　　That I didn't drink and drive,
　　Though some friends said I should.
I made a healthy choice,
　　And your advice to me was right,
　　The party finally ended,
　　And the kids drove out of sight.
I got into my car,
　　Sure to get home in one piece,
　　I never knew what was coming, Mom
　　Something I expected least.
Now I'm lying on the pavement,
　　And I hear the policeman say,
　　The kid that caused this wreck was drunk,
　　Mom, his voice seems far away.
My own blood's all around me,
　　As I try hard not to cry.
　　I can hear the paramedic say,
　　This girl is going to die.
I'm sure the guy had no idea,

While he was flying high,
Because he chose to drink and drive,
Now I would have to die.
So why do people do it, Mom
    Knowing that it ruins lives?
    And now the pain is cutting me,
    Like a hundred stabbing knives.
Tell sister not to be afraid, Mom
    Tell Daddy to be brave,
    And when I go to heaven,
    Put "Mommy's Girl" on my grave.
Someone should have taught him,
    That it's wrong to drink and drive.
    Maybe if his parents had,
    I'd still be alive.
My breath is getting shorter, Mom
    I'm getting really scared.
    These are my final moments,
    And I'm so unprepared.
I wish that you could hold me, Mom,
    As I lie here and die.
    I wish that I could say, "I love you, Mom!"
    So I love you and... good-bye.

— Author Unknown

In most places, the legal amount of alcohol a driver is allowed to have in their blood stream is .08. On average, this works out to be about one drink per one hour time frame. Make sure you stay well below this.

Be very careful about how much you and your friends drink at university parties. It is too easy to get caught up in the moment and drink more than you intended to. If you or your friends do drink, call a cab or a sober friend to drive you home. Please.

41 Extending condolences

SATURDAY

When you have to extend condolences to someone, remember, first and foremost, to be sincere. Second, if you knew the person who passed away, highlight something that impressed you about them when communicating with their loved ones.

42 The most informative textbook ever

SUNDAY

Some people say that when it comes to life lessons, the Bible is the most informative textbook you will ever read. The Christian Bible has two sections:

1. A rule book (the Old Testament) that gives rules to live by; and
2. A book of case studies (the New Testament) that illustrates how to live by offering examples.

Almost everything you need to know to live a fulfilled, virtuous life can be found in the Bible... after all, keep in mind what BIBLE stands for:

**Basic
Instructions
Before
Leaving
Earth**

43 Our greatest glory is not in never falling, but it is in rising every time we fall

MONDAY

— Confucius (551 BC–479 BC)

Too many people live their lives trying to avoid failure. They are too tentative or too afraid to try anything, and consequently they don't get far in life. While you are trying to get ahead in life, naturally there will be times when you don't succeed. Treat every fall as a chance to get up, start again and do it right the next time. This attitude will help you learn that you can recover from a failure. And you will find that the more times you get up, the easier it becomes when you have to do so again.

ATTRIBUTE OF THE STRONG

44 At work, never enter into a romantic relationship with a direct subordinate

It is a no-win situation for both of you, and there can significant professional damage if the relationship turns bad. For example, if the relationship breaks off acrimoniously, there is a possibility the subordinate may try to "get back" at you by claiming harassment.

Even prior to that, it can damage the reputation of both people. People may talk: he or she is taking advantage of their more powerful position; or one is trying to "sleep" their way to a promotion. If your relationship with a subordinate starts to develop into something more than employer/employee, arrange a transfer for one of you before anything serious occurs.

45 Business partnerships, like marriages, always start out with the best of intentions

Unfortunately, just like many marriages, business partnerships break down. Therefore, before entering into any kind of partnership, make sure to put in place a well-defined exit mechanism. The most effective mechanism is to have a written partnership agreement that includes a "shotgun" clause. Under the terms of a shotgun clause, one partner can make an offer to buy out the second partner, but upon doing so the second partner has the right to buy out the first partner at the exact same price. This ensures that the first partner makes a fair offer right at the outset, because in turn he or she could be forced to sell their shares at that price.

46 It's better to keep your mouth shut and appear stupid than to open it and remove all doubt

— *Mark Twain (1835–1910)*

If you don't know something about a topic, don't say anything. There may be times you feel compelled to comment on something you know nothing about. In those instances it is best not to say anything at all, or to say that you don't know, rather than looking foolish by pretending that you do.

47 Lending money to family can be dangerous if not done properly

FRIDAY

Money changes relationships, and often not for the good. If you are in a position to be able to lend a meaningful amount of money to a family member (brother, sister, cousin), follow these three rules:

1. Get the repayment terms in writing (or don't expect to be repaid);
2. Don't charge interest; and
3. Do it only once.

48 When traveling, drink the local wine

SATURDAY

— *Harrison McCain (1927–2004)*

When you are traveling, show respect for your host and the area or country you are visiting by trying a local delicacy. It may be wine, beer, liqueur, chocolates or a special dish. Your willingness to try the local product will show your host that you respect the local culture. That effort will undoubtedly help make your stay more comfortable.

49 When you do good deeds, don't try to show off. If you do, you won't get a reward from your Father in heaven

SUNDAY

— *Matthew 6:1*

You should want to do good things for the sake of helping someone, not for any recognition that may come your way. Give of yourself because you have the ability to give, not because you expect something in return. This way, you will never be disappointed.

50 The best way out is always through

MONDAY

— Robert Frost (1874–1963)

Avoid looking for convoluted or roundabout ways to avoid a problem. On the contrary, approach the problem head-on. The reality is that you are going to have to face it at some point anyway. Save time and energy – attack the problem immediately and get it resolved.

51 The path to the Presidency

TUESDAY

If you have hopes one day of becoming the president of your company, don't work for a family business (unless of course it is your own family). It is rare that a family member gets passed over in favor of an outsider when a senior job opens up. You may be the best candidate for the position, but blood is thicker than water and you are likely to be disappointed.

52 Education is when you read the fine print. Experience is when you don't

WEDNESDAY

— Pete Seeger (b. 1919)

There is a reason why there is fine print. It is usually because someone is trying to protect themselves. If they need to do this, it is probably because something negative has happened in the past or there is a real chance of something bad happening in the future. Therefore, make sure you read the fine print. It could save you time and money.

53 It is pardonable to be defeated, but never to be surprised

THURSDAY

— Frederick the Great (1712–1786)

Being beaten – in a game, for a job, or to make a sale – will happen no matter how good you are. While it is acceptable to lose (although one hopes not too often), it is unacceptable to fail because you were not properly prepared. When entering any kind of competition – athletic, academic or business – you must be well informed and well prepared.

More specifically, in business you should never be caught by surprise. You need to develop an intelligence network so that you have a constant stream of current, relevant information. You need to know as much as possible about what your competition, customers and suppliers are doing at all times.

54 Make sure you show appreciation for any gesture of kindness

Your response does not have to be anything "flashy." Small gestures can be just as meaningful as something much bigger, so don't feel you have to go overboard with your thanks. Giving a single rose is as good as giving a dozen roses – it is the thought that counts.

55 What plate is mine?

When you attend a large social function or a business conference, there may be a sit-down meal. If so, you may find you are seated at a round table that is too small for the number of people, making it quite crowded. In these instances, keeping track of your own dishes may be difficult. You don't want to use somebody else's dinnerware, so keep in mind that your drinking glass is on your right and your bread plate is on your left. An easy way to remember this is to consider the first two letters of each word: drink, dr = drink right; and plate, pl = plate left.

...WE MUST LOSE OUR FEAR OF BEING WRONG

56 Nothing more can be considered as real merit for a person than his effort. Only in his effort is a person shown in his real light

— The Koran

Always put forward your best effort. You will be judged more often on your effort than on the result.

As harsh as it sounds, there will always be someone who has more natural talent than you have (or for that matter, more strength, speed, good looks or brains). Accept the fact that these lucky individuals are out there and that you will be competing against them. Regardless of their advantages, you can overcome not being the biggest, fastest, smartest or best-looking. You can do it by working hard.

Understand also that strength, speed, good looks and mental ability usually fade over time. People who have relied on their natural talent to get ahead have often not learned what it takes to be successful in the long run: hard work.

Now, if you are one of those lucky ones who do possess speed, strength, good looks or brains, make sure you add the most important quality to your skill set: work ethic. Employers usually attribute more importance to a person's work ethic than to their talent. A healthy work ethic is one quality you are not born with. It must be developed.

57 Don't be afraid to go out on a limb. That's where the fruit is

— H. Jackson Brown, Jr.

In other words: "no guts, no glory." You need to be prepared to take some chances in life in order to get some rewards. You will find that most of the things generally considered important – love, success, education, wealth – will require you to risk something in order to achieve. If you risk nothing, the achievement often won't mean as much.

58 Looking Good

In public speaking, good body language is very important, regardless of the number of people in the audience. Whether in front of fifty people or one person, there are five aspects of body language to be conscious of: posture, gestures, body movements, facial expressions and eye contact.

Posture: you should always stand up straight (but not rigid). When standing still and talking to people, your feet should be six to twelve inches apart. Stand on the balls of your feet and lean forward just a little. Your knees should be straight but not locked. Hold your chest up and stomach in. Relax your shoulders but don't let them droop. Your head should be erect and your chin up. Try to look relaxed.

Gestures: any gestures should reinforce what you are saying and are usually made with your hands or arms. To be effective, the gestures should be relevant, purposeful, and, if speaking to a larger group of people, easily visible. As well, any gestures must mean the same thing to your audience as they mean to you. Be careful you don't inadvertently insult someone with a gesture because it means something different to you than it does to your audience.

Body movements: If you are making a presentation, be sure to change your position or location during your speech. This is done for a few reasons: moving will often support or reinforce what you say; it will attract attention, thereby keeping your audience focused on you; and it will disperse tension. You should never move without a reason, however, in order not to distract your listeners.

Facial expressions: Understand that your face, more than any other part of your body, communicates your emotions, attitudes and feelings. No facial expressions = no feeling. An audience tends to mirror a speaker's facial expressions. Thus, if you smile, they smile; if you frown, they frown.

Eye Contact: Eye contact brings people into what you are saying. A good presenter tries to make any speech seem like a normal conversation. By looking your audience in the eyes, they perceive you seeing them as individuals. This helps to convince them that you are sincere and that you are interested in them. Making eye contact also does two other things: first, it helps to overcome any nervousness, because now you are looking at the audience as individuals rather than as something unknown; second, it gives you feedback and helps you to make immediate adjustments in your comments.

59 To be a great leader, you have to be PICDD

There are five traits you need to possess to be an effective leader:

Passion: you must be very committed to your cause.

Integrity: you must have a strong ethical foundation.

Communication: you must be able to communicate effectively.

Discipline: you must have the discipline to keep focused on your goal.

Decisiveness: you must be able to make a decision.

60 Take a rest; a field that has rested gives a bountiful crop

— Ovid (43 BC–17 AD)

Ovid said this 2,000 years ago and it is even more relevant today. Today's world is chaotic and fast-paced. The internet and the 24/7 culture has resulted in an unprecedented speeding-up of our lives.

If you continually try to keep up, you will burn out. It is important – indeed, necessary – for you to take time to relax and recharge your batteries on a regular basis.

61 Learn the words to at least one famous poem

FRIDAY

An ability to recite a poem shows that you are cultured and worldly. Don't be a show-off, but if you can, learn a couple of poems that you can recite in different social settings. *The Cremation of Sam McGee* by Robert Service makes a great story around a fireplace or campfire (although it's very long). Christopher Marlowe's *The Passionate Shepherd to His Love* is a great poem to recite to that special someone in your life (or whom you want to be in your life). The *23rd Psalm* is helpful in times of loneliness or despair.

62 Talk to me

SATURDAY

An important aspect of being a good conversationalist is showing sincere interest in the person you are talking to and in what they have to say. Be an active listener: listen with your ears, eyes and whole face. Active listening includes things such as making eye contact, nodding, smiling, laughing, asking relevant questions, and having an open and receptive body language.

63 Unless you are faithful in the little things, you won't be faithful in the big things

SUNDAY

— Luke 16:10

As difficult as it may be sometimes, avoid taking shortcuts or telling "little" lies. Shortcuts or small lies have a way of being found out. And when your boss, professor, spouse or friend finds out, they will tend to think that, if you were prepared to tell little lies, it is in your character to tell bigger ones as well.

...AND OTHERS WILL RESPECT YOU

64 Sometimes it may seem that hard work does not pay off, but it usually does in the long run

Consider the growth pattern of a bamboo tree.

On day one, a bamboo seed is planted in the ground. It is watered and fertilized for a year. There is no growth. It is watered and fertilized for another year: no growth. The same thing happens in years three and four: no growth. In the fifth year, it is watered and fertilized – and it grows twenty feet.

During the first four years, all of the growth is underground. You don't see any outward growth because it is expending all its energy in setting up an extensive root system. Once the roots are set, it grows extremely fast.

Keep this in mind when you are trying to build something of lasting value – a business, a team, a relationship or your career. Adopt the mentality that your hard work is fertilizing the roots of your success. Don't be discouraged by the apparent lack of "above-the-ground" growth in the early days; success will come once the roots are strong.

65 Speaking to an audience

At some point in your life, you will be required to speak to an audience. It may be ten people in a boardroom, fifty people in your psychology class, or two hundred people at your wedding. Regardless of the size of the audience, you will need to be prepared. Here are some general principles to keep in mind when speaking to an audience:

1. **Stand up** – when you do, you look taller, more authoritative and more energetic;
2. **Adjust your language to the audience** – make sure your terminology is appropriate to your audience, and never tell off-color jokes or use swear words;
3. **Don't read from a text** – it's boring;
4. **Speak with passion and enthusiasm** – if you aren't enthusiastic,

the audience will be insulted because they will think you do not want to be there (this is especially true for speeches at your wedding);

5. **Don't ramble on or repeat yourself needlessly** – work from an outline;

6. **Take your time when speaking**, but don't go so slow that you bore people. Make sure your words are clear and coherent, and don't race through the speech;

7. **Have a structure to your comments:** an opening, a body and a conclusion; and

8. **If the audience does not know you**, try to find something in common with them; people like people with whom they can identify.

66 Wearing a name tag

WEDNESDAY

When you attend a business event or social gathering at which you are asked to wear a name tag, always pin it to your right lapel. Since we customarily shake hands with the right hand, putting the name tag on the right side places it directly in front of the person you are meeting, making it easier for them to see it and learn your name. When you say your name and they notice it on your name tag, they will be more likely to remember you.

67 Reprove a friend in secret, but praise him before others

THURSDAY

— *Leonardo da Vinci (1452–1519)*

Substitute the word colleague, teammate or loved one for friend.

No one likes to be criticized – even less so when it happens in public. Therefore, don't be critical in public. If you need to offer some constructive criticism, make sure it is done the proper way: in private and with a positive message attached to it. Constructive criticism must possess two things: first, it must be seen by the recipient to be helpful; and two, it cannot be delivered as a personal attack.

On the other side of the coin, people like to be praised in public. They enjoy being made to look good in front of an audience. This is not to say that you should not compliment someone in private, but you can create goodwill by publicly broadcasting their good deeds. They will appreciate it.

68 Don't borrow things

Never borrow something breakable from your friends or neighbors. The reason is simple: if you do borrow something and you break it, you will have to buy a new one. You would have been better off buying the item for yourself at the outset.

69 Strive to show class

Class is the ability to make people feel comfortable in any type of situation.

To exemplify class, develop the ability to **CICC** (pronounced "kick"): Convey Interest, Concern and Caring. If you can **CICC** in any situation, with anyone and without being phony about it, you've got class.

70 Facing difficult times in your life

There will be times in life when challenges will seem too difficult to handle. These could be challenges faced at college, in your job, in your marriage, or with your kids. With any luck, during those tough times you will have a loved one nearby to help and support you. However, sometimes they may not be near for geographical, emotional or financial reasons. Those are times when you need someone else to lean on. Keep in mind Psalm 55:22 of the Bible during those times.

"Cast your burdens upon the Lord and he will sustain you." – Psalm 55:22

71 Don't let fear cause you to fail

MONDAY

To illustrate how fear can lead to poor performance, consider this story.

The Balance Beam

One of the last drills the varsity basketball coach would have players do on the first day of tryouts was to walk across a gymnastics balance beam. The coach would start the drill by saying that, if they made it across the beam without falling off, they would be allowed to come back the next day. If they fell off, however, they were cut from the team. The players figured the drill was designed to test their balance, an important skill in basketball.

Everybody could walk the beam with no problem.

On the second day, the coach would ask everybody to do it again. However, he would make one change that would result in no one wanting to try it, even though it meant they would not make the team.

What was the difference between the two days? On the first day, the balance beam was set at its normal height: three feet off the ground. On the second day, the beam was suspended from the ceiling of the gymnasium, about fifty feet off the ground. It was the same beam and the same width, but no one was willing to try to walk across it – even though the day before they had done it with no problem. The difference was that they were now afraid. Fear took control.

Of course, in reality the coach didn't cut anybody for not making the attempt. He used it to illustrate that sometimes fear causes you to avoid trying things you know you can do.

MEDICINE

...IT IS CHEAP

This is not to say that you should be foolish about taking risks, especially if there is a possibility of physical harm. However, don't let fear stop you from doing the things you know you can do.

72 Firing someone

During your career, there will be times when you will have to let an employee go – for disciplinary, competency or economic reasons. Regardless of the cause, always have a witness in the room with you. This is especially true if the person you are letting go is a member of the opposite sex. Although most employees have an idea that bad news is coming, it is still an emotional experience. People may react by retaliating in different ways – verbally, physically and even legally – after the fact. Because of the potential for these types of responses, you should always have a witness in the room when you talk to the employee. This reduces the likelihood of retaliation toward you personally, and helps protect the company from frivolous or trumped-up charges of misconduct.

73 The greatest leaders tend to lead by example

This can be done in two ways: first, by being prepared to do some dirty work; and second, by cultivating the belief that you would not ask someone to do something you were not prepared to do yourself. In either case, you gain the respect of your subordinates and your superiors.

When adopting this philosophy, however, you will need to be careful about how you allocate your time. A leader is paid to lead, not wash the floors. Nevertheless, it is important to lead by example in some noteworthy way. This may mean you have to get your hands dirty every once in a while.

74 What to call your elders

THURSDAY

No matter what your age, always call your elders or your superiors "Mr.," "Mrs.," "Ms.," "Sir" or "Ma'am" until they tell you otherwise. It is polite and shows respect.

75 Take your time

FRIDAY

There's a carpenter's proverb that says "measure twice, cut once." Once you cut a piece of wood, you cannot make it longer again if you have made a mistake. Make sure you consider your actions before you begin something, as you may not be able to go back and fix things.

76 A meal is more than just eating

SATURDAY

A meal, whether one-on-one or with a group of people, can be an effective tool in advancing your career or social network. A lot can be learned about other people (colleagues, superiors, clients) in a social setting that is away from a structured business environment.

Regardless of the reason for the meal, always be on your best behavior and show proper manners.

If the meal is business-related, here are some things to keep in mind:
1. Don't jump right into business talk: get the other person talking about his or herself.
2. Don't be late: being late says that you don't value the other person's time.
3. Don't talk religion or politics, or too much about your family: religion and politics can be inflammatory, and your family can be boring.
4. Don't dominate the conversation: be a listener.
5. Don't dawdle over ordering or eating: be decisive.
6. Don't drink alcohol at lunch or have more than one or two glasses of wine for dinner.

7. Don't fight over the bill: the person who extended the invitation pays the bill, unless that person is outnumbered by you and your colleagues, in which case you should offer to pay.

8. Don't forget your manners.

9. Don't forget to show appreciation; they are taking time to be with you.

10. Don't be extravagant; nobody likes a show-off.

77 Everything on earth has its own time and its own season

— Ecclesiastes 3:1

Patience is important.

Understand that some things – relationships, job advancements, reputations – take time to develop. Don't get stressed out if things are not moving as quickly as you would like, or if the outcome is not what you desired. If you lay the proper foundation, it will work out.

Life tends to go in cycles. There will be times when you'll be up, and times when you'll be down. When you're down, don't worry. Be patient. Work hard and eventually things will change.

78 You miss 100% of the shots you don't take

— Wayne Gretzky (b. 1961)

Remember that no one has scored a goal, sunk a basket, or thrown for a touchdown without first attempting to do it. If you don't at least try to do something, nothing is going to happen.

79 Perception is reality

Understand that what people perceive about you will be what they believe about you. Because of this, you need to be very careful about how your actions or words are perceived. Try to avoid situations that "look" wrong – even if your intentions are noble. For example, if you invite a business colleague of the opposite sex for lunch, and it is strictly business, choose an appropriate restaurant and seating arrangement. Choosing a restaurant known for its "romantic" setting, or choosing to sit in a secluded corner, may cause the meeting to be construed as something other than business.

Be very careful about putting yourself in compromising situations or situations that don't "look" right. Understand that people often think the worse. Be sure your actions appear correct; this way it is unlikely they will be perceived in the wrong light.

80 Beat your boss (to work)

In order to make a good impression, it's a good idea to make a habit of arriving at work before your boss, and leaving after him or her. Understandably, there will be times when this is not possible, but try to nurture this perception. Every employer values a healthy work ethic. If you can combine work ethic with competency, you will be well regarded.

81 There is a difference between prominence and significance

— *Rick Warren (b. 1954)*

Neither fame nor success automatically makes you important.

Significance is defined as "the quality of being important." Prominence means "to be widely known or conspicuous." Strive to be significant to your family, your company and your church. But don't confuse being significant with being prominent – they are nowhere near the same thing.

...YOU KNOW MORE THAN YOU THINK YOU DO

82 Explaining mistakes

When you make a mistake and need to explain how or why it happened, don't make excuses for the error. Rather, offer reasons for it. An excuse is an explanation that tries to remove blame from the explainer, and it shows weakness. In contrast, a reason explains how the mistake occurred and shows that you are taking ownership of the situation. This quality is valued in a person.

83 It is helpful to know a little bit about wine

However, avoid being pretentious about your wine knowledge. Here, as in everything, nobody likes a show-off.

At a minimum, you should know that there are two types of wine glasses: typically, white wine glasses are smaller and have a narrower shape; and red wine glasses are bigger and rounder so that the red wine can "breathe." White wine should be slightly chilled; red wine should be at room temperature. Be sure to sip your wine and drink slowly.

84 Practice these things. Devote your life to them so that everyone can see your progress

— *1 Timothy 4:15*

No athlete, musician or actor makes it to the professional ranks without years of practice. Even when they do make it to the top, they have to keep practicing in order to stay there. If you want to become good at something, you must be prepared to practice – and to be the best, you have to practice as much as the best.

85 Success is a journey, not a destination

MONDAY

Naturally, everyone wants to be successful. But what does "successful" mean? There are as many different definitions as there are people.

Regardless of how other people define success, expect your own definition to change over your lifetime: early on, it might be about making the honor roll in high school; later, it may be about getting into graduate school; even later, it will be about moving up the corporate ladder; and eventually, if you have kids, it will be about raising healthy, well-adjusted children.

Understand that your goals and dreams will change continually throughout your life, and that the road to success has no end.

Regardless of your definition of success, to paraphrase Robert Duvall, "Not every successful person is a good parent. But every good parent is a successful person."

When it comes to judging your success, make sure to measure it against the right criteria.

86 Keep your workspace clean and tidy

TUESDAY

Cleanliness and tidiness indicate an organized and disciplined person.

There may be times when you are buried under a ton of paperwork and time constraints make it necessary to leave your desk as it is rather than cleaning it up before you go home. Try to keep these times to a minimum.

Notwithstanding these exceptions, your office space should always be kept clean under these three scenarios:

1. If the public can see your desk, it must be tidy. Your work area is a reflection of your company;
2. Before you leave for the weekend, clean off your desk. It's nice to return to work on Monday and start the week with a clean and ordered work space; and

LAUGHTER IS

3. When you leave for a vacation, business trip or any kind of extended period, clean off your desk. You don't want your paperwork left in the open for others to read while you're gone.

87 Dress the part

WEDNESDAY

Part of being viewed as successful in business is to be sure you dress the part. In a business environment, remember the following:

Men: shoes should be kept shined; the color of your socks should serve as a bridge from your shoes to your pants; tuck in your shirt; always wear a belt; the bottom of your tie should reach your belt (when standing); you should use a tie clip to keep your tie in place; and your shirt collars should be crisp.

Women: no open-toed shoes; no short skirts; no cleavage; no exposed skin between your knees and your upper chest; and minimal, if any, makeup.

88 Reading is fun

THURSDAY

An ability to read quickly, and also to digest and understand what you have just read, will help you both at university and at work. These abilities will help reduce late-night "cramming."

The ability to read quickly is a by-product of being a voracious reader. Although it matters little what the material is – fiction, non-fiction, magazines or newspapers – the more you read, the faster you will read. Try to read for pleasure for at least one hour per day.

You also need to be able to digest and understand what you are reading. If it is important that you comprehend what you are reading – as opposed to simply reading for pleasure – go **SIRF**ing.

SIRFing is a checklist that will help you better understand and absorb the subject matter. The checklist is as follows:

Subject: ask yourself what the piece is about.

Information: consider what relevant information is discussed.

Response: ask yourself what your response is to what is presented – do you agree with it? Why or why not?

File: ask yourself if the information is worth keeping. If so, file it away (in the back of your mind or in hard copy).

89 How to become a millionaire

It is never too early to start saving for retirement. In fact, the earlier you start, the better. The compounding effect of your early savings can be substantial. By way of example, let's look at the effect of saving the equivalent of $300 per month (about $10 per day) starting at three different times in your life.

Assume you start with $0 and invest $300 per month ($3,600 per year) in a tax-sheltered account that gives you a 7.5% compounded annual return. There are a couple of types of investments you can choose to try to get at least the 7.5% average annual return. The Toronto Stock Exchange Composite Index had a 10.51% average annual return since 1960 to December 31, 2006. The Long-term Canada Bond Index has had a 9.02% return over the same period.

If you start investing $300 per month at age 22, and you get at least a 7.5% average annual return, you will be a millionaire by the time you are 65. If you start at 35, you will have $385,000; if you start at 45, you will have a measly $161,000.

Below is a table showing the results:

STARTING AGE	22	35	45
Total deposits	$154,800	$108,000	$72,000
Growth in value	$908,000	$277,000	$89,000
ACCUMULATED VALUE	$1,062,800	$385,000	$161,000

Note that the amount of money you actually deposit is not really that much different: if you start at 45, you will be have deposited $72,000 by the time you are 65; if you start at 22, you will have deposited $155,000 – a little more than double.

The reason for the big difference in value at the end of the three examples is the fact that you started saving early, and as a result received more "return on your return." This is called the "compounding effect." When you begin to invest early, you earn money on the returns you made on your initial investment, i.e., your money earns money. The beauty of compounding returns is that your money works for you, rather than you working for it.

90 Don't be afraid to give a compliment when one is warranted

But don't give one if it is not, because you will be perceived as being a "phony" or a "suck-up." Keep these guidelines in mind when you give a compliment:

1. **Be sincere:** a phony compliment does more damage than good.
2. **Be specific:** say exactly what is nice.
3. **Be unqualified:** don't qualify it by referring to the person's past history.
4. **Don't compare:** don't refer to anyone or anything else.

91 What is desirable in a man is his loyalty

— Proverbs 19:22

People value loyalty. Employers often overlook qualities such as brains and beauty (whether too little or too much!) if someone is a good "company person." Loyalty is desirable; therefore, make sure it is one of the qualities you bring to your job.

92 If the Creator had a purpose in equipping us with a neck, he surely meant us to stick it out

— Arthur Koestler (1905–1983)

It is believed that the phrase "stick your neck out" originates from the Middle Ages practice of cutting off people's necks with a guillotine or axe if they made the king unhappy or went against his commands. With a downside like this, no wonder people were afraid to do anything too radical!

Compare that downside with the social-security safety net we have today. We have the greatest access to housing, education and health care now than at any time in our history; we have unemployment insurance and pensions; we have food banks and shelters. In comparison with risk-taking in historical times, the downside today doesn't really even factor. What are the consequences today if we fail? – pretty low in comparison to past times. So don't be afraid to stick your neck out.

93 Introducing a speaker

Here are some guidelines for properly introducing a speaker.

Do NOT begin by saying they "need no introduction." Every speaker deserves a thoughtful and helpful introduction.

Generally, an introduction should undertake the following:
1. Introduce the speaker to the audience;
2. Establish a bond between the audience and the speaker; and
3. Be short, lasting less than two or three minutes long.

A good introduction is comprised of three sections:
1. **The opening**, which grabs the audience's attention and makes them aware of the importance of the upcoming subject;
2. **The body**, which explains one of the following: why this subject, why this speaker, why this audience, why at this time; and
3. **The conclusion**, which introduces the speaker by highlighting his or her expertise, and sets the mood for the audience.

94 You cannot shake hands with a closed fist

WEDNESDAY

— Indira Gandhi (1917–1984)

Expect to take part in numerous negotiations during your career. In every negotiation, there will be disagreement. However, by the time the negotiation is finished, those disputes should be over.

Many people believe there has to be a winner and a loser in all negotiations. This is not true. The best negotiations result in two winners. However, in order for this to happen, both parties will have to make compromises. Importantly, neither party can be seen to be a "loser." Both need to feel they have won.

Thus, when you do reach an agreement – which likely means that compromises have been made – be satisfied with the result and don't have regrets. Indira Gandhi's words ring true: if you have resolved the dispute or finalized the negotiations, accept the result with no ill feelings and move forward.

95 Challenge yourself to learn something new from everyone you meet

THURSDAY O_2

By adopting the stance that you want to learn something new from every person you meet, two positives will occur: first, of course, you will learn something new; and second, you will add to your network by gaining an acquaintance (and maybe even a friend).

Because of your perceived interest in them (remember, you are trying to learn something from them), the other person will likely view you as interesting because of your enthusiasm. A show of interest usually results in a lively conversation and good feelings toward one another.

96 Those that see skeletons in the closet have the most to hide

— German proverb

People who are vocal about other people's shortcomings or past mistakes, or those who make a habit of accusing people of things, often have something to hide themselves.

Avoid talking about other people's personal business, particularly if the subject is a negative one. It is unbecoming to talk about other people's dirty laundry, and it reflects poorly on you. People will avoid you if you gossip because of the fear that you'll talk about them when they are not around.

97 Table manners about dropped items

If you drop your knife, fork or piece of food onto the floor while eating, you should not put it back on the table after you have picked it up. In the case of a dropped knife or fork, ask for a new one if you are in a restaurant. If you are in someone's home, it is possible the host will offer you a new one; but if they don't, discreetly wipe it off with your napkin. If it's your napkin that you drop onto the floor, excuse yourself as you lean down, pick it up, put it back on your lap and continue eating.

98 A good name is to be more desired than great wealth

— Proverbs 22:1

Wealth will come and go. However, you have your name for life.

A good reputation can open many doors for you and your family. On the other hand, a bad reputation can keep many doors shut. Work diligently to create and preserve a good reputation. Your best asset is your good name.

...WONDERFUL FAIRYTALE OF ALL

Your looks, intelligence and abilities will change over time (and usually not for the better). However, if you have built a reputation for hard work and integrity, people will continue to view you favorably despite your age-related decline.

99 Opportunities are usually disguised as hard work so most people don't recognize them

— *Ann Landers (1918–2002)*

At the end of the day, there is no easy way to become successful. It requires hard work.

You must be ready and willing to work hard for what you want. If you are, when opportunities present themselves, you will be able to recognize and capitalize on them.

100 Don't let people down. Promises may get friends, but it is performance that must nurse and keep them

— *Owen Felltham (1602–1668)*

Under-promise and over-deliver. This will keep your boss happy. If you do the reverse – over-promise and under-deliver – you will develop a poor track record and reputation.

Along those lines, if you know you cannot do something, do not say you can. This is not to suggest that you should not attempt something that is a bit of a stretch – everyone should be prepared to take on challenges – it just means you should not promise to do something that you have no hope of accomplishing (this may just mean in the time frame required).

If it is within your capabilities and you say you can do it, make sure you do, at any cost. By not doing so – especially if you make a habit of this – you will lose the respect of those who are most important to you.

101 It is better to be a blind man than to see only yourself and nobody else

— *Muslehuddin Saadi (c. 1210–1291)*

Remember that you are only one person of many who make up your company, family, team or organization. Never believe that your success is due only to yourself, as there are others around you who helped you get where you are. Don't forget it. Be sure to acknowledge them, thank them and give them credit. If you don't, you likely won't repeat your success because you won't have their help the next time.

102 Life is like a box of chocolates, you never know what you're going to get

— *Winston Groom (b. 1944) in* Forrest Gump

You may think you know what to expect from your job, your professor, or a loved one, but understand that there are always surprises. Over time, you learn that you shouldn't be surprised to get surprised. Accept that things often do not go according to plan. Don't get down when this happens; surprises, both good and bad, are a fact of life.

103 Money is like manure. If you spread it around, it does a lot of good. But if you pile it up in one place, it stinks to high heaven

— *Clint Murchison Jr. (1923–1987)*

Money is good. The pursuit of wealth has contributed to the highest standard of living in human history. However, understand that with money comes responsibility. If you are fortunate enough to have money, share it. Keep enough for your needs and spread the rest around to make someone else's life better.

Money magnifies a person's qualities and values. The more money you have, the greater the magnification. Make sure the magnifying glass is kind to you.

104 Never speak badly about anyone, even if other people try to get you to do so

SATURDAY

Some people enjoy passing on negative comments or gossip about others – even better for them is if they can say someone else started it. Gossiping will have a detrimental effect on you at work and in your social circle. Inevitably, whoever is gossiped about eventually hears about it. This can result in any future interaction between the two of you being awkward, if not downright hostile.

A second reason to avoid speaking badly about other people is that, by doing so, you become known as a person who talks negatively about other people behind their backs. This does not make for a good reputation, and can result in a shrinking circle of friends and a reduced business and social network.

105 'For I know the plans I have for you,' declares the Lord, 'plans to prosper you and not to harm you, plans to give you hope and a future'

— *Jeremiah 29:11*

There will be times when you feel things are not going according to your plan. You get cut from the team, you don't do well on a series of exams, you lose your job, or you flunk out of university. When something like that happens, you might feel like a failure. Take comfort from the knowledge that God has a plan for all of us. And rest assured that the plan is a good one.

106 A man is not finished when he is defeated. He is finished when he quits

— Richard Nixon (1913–1994)

Accept the reality that in life there will be losses to go along with your wins. Expect to lose some games, or to miss out on a great job, or to be stood up by your date, or any number of other things that don't go your way. The reality is that in life you may have more setbacks than you do successes. When you do face a setback, don't quit.

The Stock Broker

A successful stock broker at Midland Walwyn had a great attitude about rejection. Early on in his career, he built his client list by making a lot of telephone "cold calls." He was relentless on the phone. He would make call after call and seemingly become more energized with each rejection. When asked what kept him going despite all the rejections, he responded that marketing studies had shown that, on average, for every ten cold calls made, there will be one successful call. Therefore, he took the approach that for every time he was told "no," he was one telephone call closer to being told "yes."

That attitude is a great example of how to approach setbacks.

Develop the philosophy that for each setback you experience, you are one step closer to success.

107 Gentlemen, we are all up to our necks in manure so nobody splash

— Pierre Laval (1883–1945)

When you find yourself in a bad situation, relax. Don't be vocal, don't blame others, and don't try to run from the situation. Conduct yourself in a calm manner, develop a plan, and take measured steps to try to get out of the "manure."

...TO FOLLOW THROUGH

108 Work at improving your EI

There are two kinds of intelligence: mental intelligence and emotional intelligence (EI).

Mental intelligence is your "brain power" – how well you do in school, how quickly you can understand things, etc. While mental intelligence (often referred to as IQ) is not necessarily a prerequisite for success, it sure helps to be smart. You will find that most business, academic and spiritual leaders are usually bright, well-read individuals. You will also find that these leaders exhibit higher levels of another kind of smarts: emotional intelligence (EI).

EI has been defined as the ability to monitor one's own and others' feelings and emotions and discriminate among them, and to use this information to guide one's thinking and action. In simple terms, it is about being able to do two things: being able to perceive emotions and to understand them. John Mayer and Peter Salovey[1] define EI as the capacity to understand emotional information and to reason with emotions. They talk about four areas of emotional intelligence:

1. The capacity to accurately perceive emotions;
2. The capacity to use emotions to facilitate thinking;
3. The capacity to understand emotional meanings; and
4. The capacity to manage emotions.

In essence, EI is the ability to recognize a feeling as it is happening – that you are getting angry, or vengeful, or gossipy, for example – and being able to control that emotion. In other words, it is self-awareness. Not to be confused with self-absorption, in which you care only about your own feelings, self-awareness is the ability to understand your emotions and how they are being perceived by others.

Employers are increasingly using EI tests as part of the recruiting and promotion process. Accordingly, it is very important to gain some insight into your own EI. Work diligently to improve it. You can do this by examining how you react to certain situations, especially emotional ones. Develop an ability to step outside your body and view your responses from the perspective of others.

109 Go to WAR

THURSDAY

Whenever possible, take every opportunity to go to **WAR**.

By this we mean working **a r**oom[2]. The ability to effectively circulate in a room full of people will help you broaden your social and business network. The more people you know, the more opportunities you will enjoy.

To be effective at **war**, think of yourself as a host rather than as a guest. The host is always concerned with the comfort of others and therefore tries to put others at ease. Don't go overboard – you don't want to upset the actual host – but nevertheless adopt the mindset that you will be gracious to everyone as you work to convey that you care about their well-being.

110 Being powerful is like being a lady. If you have to tell people you are, you aren't

FRIDAY

— *Margaret Thatcher (b. 1925)*

If you have to announce that you are successful (or, for that matter, powerful or rich), then in reality you are not. Arrogance often masks weakness.

111 Parlez-vous anglais?

SATURDAY

While English is spoken in most countries around the world, when travelling to a foreign country don't automatically assume that people speak English. When in a non-English-speaking country, it is a good idea to know a few words or phrases in the local language. At minimum, you should learn how to say the following: *hello, please, thank you, goodbye, excuse me, can you help me?* and *do you speak English?*

112 Adversity pursues sinners, but the righteous will be rewarded with prosperity

SUNDAY

— Proverbs 13:21

Make good choices. Live your life the right way and you will be rewarded – it may be with good health, a high standard of living, strong family relationships, or the joy of parenthood. If you are really lucky, you will be blessed with them all.

113 Genius is 1% inspiration and 99% perspiration *and* I start where the last man left off

MONDAY

— Thomas Edison (1847–1931)

Thomas Edison's invention of the light bulb has to be considered one of the three or four most important inventions in history.

Apparently, it took him more than 2,000 trials before he got the light bulb to work. This perseverance shows that he was not only a contender when it came to scientific smarts, but also in the persistence department. How different would our lives be today if he had stopped after experiment number 50, or 500 or 1,999? Make sure that when you come up against an obstacle, you pull an Edison. That is, keep trying.

114 You can view your own drawbacks only through the eyes of other people

TUESDAY

— Chinese Proverb

Every once in a while, you need to make an accounting of your strengths and weaknesses to ensure you have the necessary skills to keep yourself moving up the corporate ladder.

Unfortunately, most people cannot accurately determine their own strengths and weaknesses. Because of this shortcoming, when you want to find out what you do or don't do well, ask your superior for help. If they care about you and want you to improve, they will be candid and tell you. But be prepared to hear both the good and the bad, as painful as that may be. Once you know, capitalize on your strengths and work on correcting your weaknesses.

115 Carry yourself with confidence

When walking, walk quickly and with purpose. Quickness conveys energy and enthusiasm. Walking slowly and dragging your feet implies disinterest or apathy, something no employer wants to see.

If you wish to convey energy, enthusiasm and warmth when talking over the telephone, stand up and smile while you are talking.

116 Getting out of an awkward situation

When in an awkward situation in which someone is asking you a question you don't want to answer, ask questions back. This will put them on the defensive and give you time to properly formulate your response.

Simple questions like "Why do you want to know?", "Who asked you to ask me that?" or "How do you think I should answer that?" may be enough to deflect further probing.

117 Don't point fingers

When something goes wrong, you should never point a finger at someone else. Remember that when you do, you have three fingers pointing right back at you.

When mistakes are made, there are usually legitimate reasons. If you were part of the problem, be prepared to own up to your involvement. Don't try to pass off the blame. You may think you can deflect the blame by pointing a finger at someone else, but this usually only works once, or maybe twice. People catch on quickly. Then you not only look bad because you are trying to lay blame elsewhere, but you also create animosity. When a mistake is made, consider whether you might have had a part in it. If you did, be prepared to own up to your responsibility.

118 Viruses are all around us

Nary a day goes by that we don't hear of some kind of computer virus, flu pandemic or new strain of disease.

But there is a type of virus you don't hear very much about but that is actually more prevalent than any of the others: the lousy manners virus (particularly when driving). This virus is everywhere – try not to catch it. In fact, fight it by showing good manners. People will remember you for it.

119 Let the process go on until your endurance is fully developed, and you will find that you have become men of mature character... with no weak spots

> — *James 1:3-4*

No matter what you do, see it right through to its end. Persevere. Most of the time the lesson is learned while you are struggling to finish the task, rather than after you've finished it.

120 Those who say it cannot be done need to get out of the way of those who are doing it

> — *Confucius (551 BC–479 BC)*

Many people have an outlook that is more negative than positive. They tend to see the glass as always half empty. Expect to have to deal with people who say that something can't be done, or that it is too tough or too difficult. Don't listen to them. Be one of the people who say that something can be done... and go out and do it.

121 Every group or organization has its own culture

When you become involved in a company, organization, team or association, try to determine what the culture is as soon as possible. A company's culture is the personality or character of the company. It includes such things as core values and beliefs, ethics and behavior. It also includes other things such as dress code, work hours, leadership style, internal communication methods and work/life balance. You can get a feel for the culture by observing the most senior people and the longest-term employees.

If the culture fits with your beliefs and you can see yourself being involved on a long-term basis, try to embrace the culture as soon as possible. If the culture doesn't fit with your beliefs, cut your losses and get out quickly.

122 Sit with strangers

If you attend a conference or seminar and there is a sit-down meal, try to sit with people you do not know. This gives you the opportunity to meet someone new. By doing this, you will broaden your business network; this will help accelerate your career growth.

123 Going to a party

When you attend a party or event – be it business, personal, educational or political in nature – keep in mind the following:

1. **Adopt a positive attitude.** A negative attitude will usually embarrass someone: yourself, your employer, your kids or your spouse. Be positive or don't go.

2. **Focus on the benefit of the event**. Some benefits will be more easily discernible than others, but every get-together will usually prove to have some value if you search for it. Fundraisers, political rallies or study groups have obvious perks; a birthday party for your boyfriend's cousin does not. That is, until you find out that the cousin is a math major and can help you with your calculus homework. There is always the potential to benefit from any gathering, so don't forget to look for it.

124 Attitude counts more than achievement

FRIDAY

— *Rick Warren (b. 1954)*

Make no mistake: achievement is important. Everybody needs to have success in life in order to stay positive. However, it is vital to understand that you will not be successful in everything you try. You may fall short for a number of legitimate reasons: lack of preparation; insufficient skill level; improper education; not tall enough; too tall. No matter the outcome, though, the most important aspect of any attempt is your attitude toward it. With the right attitude, you are never a loser. You might not win the fight, but you have already won the battle.

> Any coward can fight a battle when he's sure of winning; but give me the man who has the pluck to fight when he's sure of losing.
>
> – *George Eliot (1819–1880)*

125 The proper way to hold a wine glass is to grasp it by the stem

SATURDAY

When served white wine, avoid "cupping" the bowl of the glass with your hand, because your hand temperature will warm up the wine in the glass (remember that white wine is best enjoyed slightly chilled).

Red wine is served at room temperature and therefore it is acceptable to hold the glass by the bowl. However, holding a glass of red wine by the stem is also fine.

126 Choose your friends and acquaintances wisely

You *are* your peer group.

If your friends are good students, you will be as well. If your friends don't want to better themselves, you will not want to either. If you hang around with people who think that smoking weed is acceptable, you will think the same way.

It is said that, when you enter the working world, your salary will be approximately equal to the average salary of your six closest friends.

> He who walks with wise men will be wise, but the companion of fools will suffer harm.
>
> *– Proverbs 13:20*

In so many ways, your choice of friends impacts your life. Choose well.

127 Remember the story of the four-minute mile

Running a mile in under four minutes was once thought to be humanly impossible. For decades, the top runners in the world tried and failed – no one could break through that barrier. And then on May 6, 1954, one man – Roger Bannister (b. 1929) – did it. After that, all the top milers could do it. Today, even the very best high school kids can do it.

Psychological barriers can be as difficult to overcome as physical ones. If you approach a task thinking it is impossible, you are right. It will be. If you approach a task thinking you can do it, you are also right. Mankind has shown time and again that things thought impossible often turn out not to be. So erase the word "impossible" from your vocabulary. Break through the barriers and adopt the mindset that if you can visualize it, you can do it.

...ANOTHER IS GIVEN IN ITS PLACE

128 A helpful hint for making a presentation exciting

TUESDAY

When you give a speech or presentation, one helpful hint to help build excitement is to put out fewer chairs than you will need for your audience. Making a show of having to set out extra chairs gives the impression that interest in your speech is higher than expected, thus creating a "buzz" in the room prior to your opening line.

129 A leader must be able to motivate others

WEDNESDAY

To motivate people, three things must be present: first, the people need to share a similar goal as you; second, they need to accept your message; finally, they need to respect you. If people respect you as a person, they will respect you as a leader, and they will then be inclined to respect your message. To gain their respect, make sure you are personable, fair, supportive and decisive, i.e., someone who is aware of the wants and needs of his or her staff.

Avoid trying to motivate by fear – for example, by using threats, punishment or intimidation. This strategy may work, but only in the short-term. People won't work for you for very long if you use this approach.

130 Be guided by your goals, not blinded by them

THURSDAY

— *Susan Roane*

Accomplishment requires focus. Success at university, promotions at work, extra playing time on your team – all begin with having a goal in mind and then diligently working toward it. However, be careful you are not so focused on your goal that you cannot see what is happening around you. In every kind of environment, your success will require the help of colleagues, teammates, friends or classmates. Understand that those people have goals and aspirations as well, and that their goals are just as important to them as yours are to you. Make sure you remember that.

Remain focused on your goals, but be aware that other people will be watching your actions. Nobody likes blatant corporate climbers, people who monopolize the professor's attention, or someone who doesn't pass the ball. Stay aware of, and sympathetic to, the people around you.

131 Rotten wood cannot be carved

— *Chinese Proverb*

No matter how good a coach, mentor, supervisor or friend you are, if you have a person around you who is unethical or who lies or cheats, get rid of them. No matter what you do, you will not be able to effectively manage or work with them. At some point, they will reflect badly on you.

132 Table etiquette

When it comes to proper table etiquette, the basic idea to keep in mind is that you want to preserve cleanliness.

When you sit down at a table, pick up your napkin, open it up discreetly, and place it on your lap. Your napkin should not be left on the table once you have sat down. Do not tuck it into your waistband. Lay it on your lap.

If you have been invited by someone to the meal – whether at their home or at a restaurant – do not start eating until one of two things happen: either the host starts eating, or the host asks you to start eating. It is proper manners to wait for the signal, and this also avoids embarrassment should the host want to say grace and you have already started eating. At functions for which there is no designated "host," do not start eating until everyone has been served their plates and/or at least two other people have begun to eat. Again, this shows good manners and avoids the embarrassment of starting to eat when someone is planning to offer a welcome, toast or blessing.

133 I dreamed I had an interview with God

"So you would like to interview me?" God asked.

"If you have the time," I said.

God smiled. "My time is eternity. What questions do you have in mind for me?"

"What surprises you most about humankind?"

God answered. "That they get bored with childhood, they rush to grow up, and then long to be children again. That they lose their health to make money... and then lose their money to restore their health. That by thinking anxiously about the future, they forget the present, such that they live in neither the present nor the future. That they live as if they will never die, and die as though they had never lived."

God's hand took mine and we were silent for a while. And then I asked, "As a parent, what are some of life's lessons you want your children to learn?

"To learn that they cannot make anyone love them. All they can do is let themselves be loved. To learn that it is not good to compare themselves to others. To learn to forgive by practising forgiveness. To learn that it only takes a few seconds to open profound wounds in those they love, and it can take many years to heal them. To learn that a rich person is not one who has the most, but is one who needs the least. To learn that there are people who love them dearly, but simply have not yet learned how to express or show their feelings. To learn that two people can look at the same thing and see it differently. To learn that it is not enough that they forgive one another, but they must also forgive themselves."

"Thank you for your time," I said humbly. "Is there anything else you would like your children to know?"

God smiled and said, "Just know that I am here… always."

— *Author Unknown*

134 A pessimist sees the difficulty in every opportunity, an optimist sees the opportunity in every difficulty

— *Sir Winston Churchill (1874–1965)*

Mondays can be tough. In fact, without the right attitude they can be hazardous to your health. A British study conducted in the late 1990s and reported in the *British Medical Journal* examined 80,000 deaths of heart disease over a ten-year period. It found that up to 20% more people die from heart attacks on Monday than any other day[3].

Rather than being stressed out about going back to work or school on Monday, start the week with the right attitude. Approach Monday with the perspective that you are going to have a good day. Adopt the mind-set that you are going to be better off at the end of the day – because you learned something new, met someone new or accomplished something – than you were at the start of the day. Make something positive out of it. Be a Monday optimist.

135 Behold the turtle. He makes progress only when he sticks his neck out

— *Jim Bryant Conant (1893–1978)*

Sometimes you need to act like a turtle: don't be afraid to spend some time in your shell (i.e., kick back), but know that in order to get ahead you will have to stick your neck out eventually (especially in love and business).

…THAN HE WHO THINKS HIMSELF SO

136 The person who speaks much will seldom fulfill all his words in his actions. A wise person is always wary lest his words surpass his actions

— Chinese proverb

Big talkers rarely perform up to their boasts. It might be because they spend so much time talking that they don't have time to perform, or it could be because big talkers are often insecure people – when the pressure is on, often they can't do the job. Remember that actions speak louder than words.

137 A lie may fool someone else, but it tells you the truth: you're weak

— Tom Wolfe (b. 1931), The Bonfire of the Vanities.

Striving to always tell the truth builds character. Every time you do so – particularly when it is difficult – you get stronger. Every time you tell a lie to extricate yourself from a tricky situation, you lose a little something of yourself. Life is all about moving forward. Don't move backward; work to get stronger, not weaker.

138 The only really happy people are those who have learned how to serve

— Albert Schweitzer (1875–1965)

Life is full of happy occasions: when you get married, when you get a promotion, when your children are born. Unfortunately, those moments don't happen often enough. You might need to inject some happiness into your life every once in a while. One thing you can do to make yourself feel good is to help someone less fortunate than yourself. You'll find that helping others is a great "happy pill." Take as needed.

139 Introducing two people

When making introductions between two people, say the name of the person you want to show the most respect for first. Usually it is the older person.

In general, introduce older people to younger people first, and senior people to junior people.

140 Wealth obtained by fraud dwindles, but the one who gathers by labor increases it

— Proverbs 13:11.

It seems that every week the media reports on some fraudulent or illegal activity conducted by businesspeople. These stories are baffling, because many have achieved considerable success and riches only to have their wealth and reputation destroyed by their own poor behavior. When you are building your career, make sure your actions and activities are morally, ethically and legally defensible.

Equally important, keep your moral and ethical foundation intact when you reach the top. It can be a precipitous fall if you are knocked off your perch due to improper behavior.

141 The harder the conflict, the more glorious the triumph

— Thomas Jefferson (1743–1826)

You can expect to experience many achievements in your lifetime. Some may be small – acing your mid-term exam or winning the piano recital – and some will be big – making the Dean's List or earning your first million dollars. Regardless of the size of the achievement, the most satisfying ones are those that result from sacrifice and hard work.

A feeling of success is magnified by the amount of adversity that was overcome to achieve it. And one reminder: when you do reach the top, enjoy it.

142 Don't clutter your mind

TUESDAY

Albert Einstein (1879–1955) said that there is no need to clutter your mind with information you will only use occasionally; therefore, he suggested that you keep files.

One way to help remember things about people that you meet is to write the date you met them on the back of their business card, as well as something about the circumstance of the meeting, and perhaps some basic information you might have learned. If the business card is too small, you can use 3" x 5" cards, or better yet, set up electronic files in your computer or PDA. In addition to having the information available, you will find that the act of writing the items down will help you to remember them better.

143 Nothing is so contagious as enthusiasm

WEDNESDAY

— Edward Bulwer-Lytton (1803–1873)

Enthusiasm = interest. By showing enthusiasm for your job, you are telling your employer that you enjoy working for him or her. By showing enthusiasm in the classroom, you are showing your professor that you like the class. By showing enthusiasm at soccer practice, you are showing your coach and your teammates that you want to get better.

Your show of enthusiasm will stimulate others to be enthusiastic as well, for two reasons: first, they will have to show enthusiasm or risk being viewed as disinterested; and second, if it looks like you are having a good time, they will want to share in your excitement.

144 Don't measure yourself by what you have accomplished but by what you should have accomplished with your ability

— John Wooden (b. 1910)

Some people start with an advantage in life. It may be family money, access to good schools, or family connections. However, most of us don't start out with these advantages. Therefore, it is not fair to judge someone's accomplishments by looking only at where they ended up. On the contrary, consider where they started. The distance traveled gives a more accurate portrayal of their success.

145 One must forge the iron while it is hot

— German proverb

If something needs to get done, do it right away. Don't procrastinate. The best time to get something done is right now. Take action when the opportunity first presents itself. Think of it as you would if you were trying to shape cooling steel: if you wait too long, it may be more difficult – or impossible – to do.

146 It is what it is

There are people out there who are "storytellers." These people like to tell stories in order to get attention, and usually the bigger the story, the more attention they get. Don't fall into this trap. Try to avoid embellishing a story. If a story can't stand on its true facts, it means it was probably not interesting enough to tell in the first place. If you become known as an "embellisher," people will tend to discount your comments; they may even question the accuracy of other things you say.

...IMAGINATION OVER INTELLIGENCE

147 Treat people the same way you want them to treat you

— Matthew 7:12

More commonly known as the Golden Rule, this is the basis upon which you should always deal with people.

148 Success is never final. Failure is never fatal

— Sir Winston Churchill (1874–1965)

When you succeed, don't stop. When you fail, don't give up.

149 Keep your car clean

You never know when you will have to give someone you need to impress a ride – someone like your boss, a co-worker or a date. A clean and tidy car shows you are organized and that you care about how you are perceived. Keeping your car clean is even more important if you have a company vehicle. Your company car is a direct reflection of your employer, so not keeping your car clean says to your boss that you don't care how your company is viewed.

150 Be wary of certain words

During discussions or negotiations, there are certain words that people use that hint that their degree of certainty is lower than they want you to think. This is particularly true when the words or phrases are used as an introduction to a statement. For instance, phrases such as "no doubt," "of course," and "naturally" can reveal that a person is probably not as confident about their position as they would have you believe.

151 The essence of true friendship is to make allowance for another's little lapses

THURSDAY

— *David Storey (b. 1933)*

Accept the fact that your friends and loved ones are not perfect; they make mistakes. Be supportive of them and don't be critical. If you want a friendship to grow, look past mistakes, faults or transgressions. Remember that a true friend would not knowingly hurt you or cause you pain; so if something like that happens, give them the benefit of the doubt and forgive them.

152 Mortgage Payoff vs. Retirement Savings

FRIDAY

An oft-asked question when it comes to your personal financial planning is whether you should try to pay off your house mortgage as quickly as possible, or whether you should take that extra money and invest in a retirement savings plan.

The answer in either case is yes. You should do both. While in general it is important to avoid debt, a home mortgage is one exception to this rule because a home is usually an appreciating asset. Houses generally go up in value, and so it will likely always be worth more than the debt that is attached to it.

Notwithstanding this fact, it is a good idea to have a strategy to pay down your mortgage and save for retirement at the same time. The reason is that, if you use all of your funds toward paying down your mortgage, by the time it is finally paid off you may be 25 years or more into your career. You will have lost 25 years of retirement savings and the compounding effect (see Day 89) of the early savings.

This two-pronged approach is vital. For one, if your total financial plan is to pay off your mortgage, you may be tempted to go out and buy a bigger house once your goal is achieved. This bigger house is often bought with the help of another mortgage, and could cause you to delay saving for retirement even longer.

153 If you are the host of a social function, it is your responsibility to properly convey the dress code ahead of time

SATURDAY

A host should never be dressed better than his or her guests, as it could make them feel uncomfortable. If by some chance you do find yourself in this position, consider changing – but only if you can do it discreetly.

154 The 23rd Psalm

SUNDAY

The Lord is my Shepherd; I shall not want.
  He makes me lie down in green pastures:
  He leads me beside the still waters.
  He restores my soul:
  He leads me in the paths of righteousness for His name's sake.
Yea, though I walk through the valley of the shadow of death,
  I will fear no evil: For you are with me;
  Thy rod and thy staff, they comfort me.
  You prepare a table before me in the presence of mine enemies;
  You anoint my head with oil; My cup runs over.
Surely goodness and mercy shall follow me all the days of my life,
  and I will dwell in the House of the Lord forever.

155 When something is irritating or bothering you, try to be like an oyster

MONDAY

Lessons from an Oyster

There once was an oyster whose story I tell,
  Who found that some sand had got into his shell.
  It was only a grain, but it gave him great pain.
  For oysters have feelings although they are so plain.

Now, did he berate the harsh workings of fate
>That had brought him to such a deplorable state?
>Did he curse at the government, cry for election,
>And claim that the sea should have given him protection?

"No," he said to himself as he lay on a shell,
>"Since I cannot remove it, I shall try to improve it."

Now the years have rolled around, as the years always do,
>And he came to his ultimate destiny – stew.
>And the small grain of sand that had bothered him so
>Was a beautiful pearl all richly aglow.

Now the tale has a moral, for isn't it grand
>What an oyster can do with a morsel of sand?
>What couldn't we do if we'd only begin
>With some of the things that get under our skin.

— Author Unknown

156 When making a presentation, try to incorporate visual aids into it

TUESDAY

Visual aids help a presentation, for the following reasons:

1. **They increase understanding.** We live in a visual age and most of what people learn is taken in through their eyes, not their ears. We gain 75% of what we learn through our sense of sight, versus just 11% from our sense of hearing[4]. Visuals help convey messages in the way best suited to clear understanding.

2. **They save time.** Information presented visually is received and processed by the brain faster than a verbal message. Visuals are especially useful in helping people quickly understand complex or abstract ideas.

3. **They help retention.** Studies have shown that people remember

PERFECTION

...NOT

an average of just 10% of a spoken message a week after it's presented. However, they remember up to 50% of what they both see and hear[5].

4. **They promote attentiveness.** People can think much faster than you can speak, so their minds tend to wander during a speech. Visuals help keep the audience focused on your message and add some variety to your presentation. However, you should never "read" off your visuals. Your audience members can read themselves and don't want you doing it for them.

5. **They help control nervousness.** Displaying the visual gives you a valid reason to be moving around, and that lets your body deal with the nervous energy without distracting the audience.

157 A leader has to motivate people

WEDNESDAY

Monetary rewards can be a good motivator; however, studies have shown that it is usually not the best reason, and in fact ranked eleventh on a list of reasons why employees stay where they are[6]. The best motivational tool is making people feel important.

People want to feel that their input is valuable, as then they feel *they* are valuable. Making people believe they are an integral part of what you are doing is the foundation of team motivation. If people feel important to the cause, they will be motivated to do a good job.

Mary Kay Ash (1918–2001) said: "Everyone has an invisible sign hanging from their neck saying 'make me feel important.' Never forget this message when working with people."

Once you have created this feeling of importance, there are three other things that should be present to foster motivation:

1. A challenge to meet or a goal to attain;

2. A reputation to live up to (their own, the company's, the team's); and

3. The belief that they possess a unique ability to help get the job done.

158 It's easy to lose weight

The secret to losing weight is really quite simple. All you have to do is to consume fewer calories per day than what your body needs.

If you want to consume more calories per day than what your body typically needs, then you have to do something to burn off those extra calories. If you don't, you will gain weight. Consider this: one pound of fat is the approximate equivalent of 3,500 calories. Therefore, in order to lose one pound per week, you will need to consume 500 calories per day less than what your body needs. If you want to lose two pounds per week, you will need to reduce your calorie intake by 1,000 calories per day. The flip side of course, is that if you consume 3,500 calories per week more than what your body needs, you will gain one pound.

It is important to have a general idea of how many calories you may consume per day in order to remain at your steady weight. The caloric intake required to maintain a steady weight can be calculated using a formula. Below are worksheets that show approximate guidelines.

Women

Assume the following information: you are 18 years old, weigh 150 pounds, are 5'7" tall and don't do much in the way of exercise.

Multiply your weight in pounds by 4.35 and then add 655	(150 x 4.35) + 655	= 1,308
Multiply your height in inches by 4.32	67 x 4.32	= 289
Multiply your age by 4.7	18 x 4.7	= 85
Subtract the result from step 3 from the result in step 2	289 – 85	= 204
Add the result of step 4 to the result in step 1	1,308 + 204	= 1,512

In this case, the number of calories per day you could consume and continue to maintain a steady weight is approximately 1,512. Of course, if you are a physically active, you could consume more calories than this and maintain your weight.

Men

Assume the following information: you are 18 years old, weigh 190 pounds, and are 5'11" tall and relatively sedentary.

Multiply your weight in pounds by 6.22 and then add 660	(190 x 6.22) + 660	= 1,842
Multiply your height in inches by 12.7	71 x 12.7	= 902
Multiply your age by 6.8	18 x 6.8	= 122
Subtract the result from step 3 from the result in step 2	902 – 122	= 780
Add the result of step 4 to the result in step 1	1,842 + 780	= 2,622

In this case, the number of calories per day you can consume and keep a steady weight is approximately 2,622. Remember that the more you exercise, the more you can eat.

There are a number of online calorie calculators that can do the above calculation quickly for you. Just type in "calorie calculator" on any search engine.

159 When it comes to money, develop gas

Develop the mentality that **g**iving **and s**aving are more important than spending. Saving money gives you financial stability. Giving money gives you emotional stability. All spending gives you is a smaller bank account.

Spending your money – other than for the essentials such as food, shelter, clothing, etc. – may make you feel happy today, but you'll find that the feel-good effect does not last long. Soon, you'll have to spend more to get the feeling again. If you want to feel great, do it by giving and saving: **gas.**

160 Mouth manners

When you have to remove something inedible from your mouth – seeds, bones, etc. – the general rule is that it should be taken out the same way it went in. For example, olive pits can be delicately dropped into your open palm before putting them onto your plate, and a piece of gristle or bone from chicken should be dropped discreetly onto your fork and then returned to the plate. The only exception to this rule is fish. It is acceptable to remove the tiny bones with your fingers, as they are too difficult to drop from your mouth onto the fork. If you do have to spit out something that is large and unattractive, discreetly spit it into your napkin so you can keep it out of sight.

161 My temptations have been my masters in divinity

— Martin Luther (1483–1546)

Resisting temptation is an education in itself. Every day you can expect to be faced with some kind of temptation. In school – to take shortcuts when completing assignments; at work – to not put in a full day's work for a full day's pay; in your love life – well, there are a lot of attractive people out there. Do not feel bad that you are tempted. Rather, adopt the attitude that it is simply another challenge to overcome. And remember – the more challenges you overcome, the stronger you become.

162 Fortune favors the brave

— Virgil (70 BC–19 BC)

Whether in business or in love, be prepared to take chances. Just make sure that the chances you take are carefully considered and are not foolish ones.

163 Be sure to enjoy your job

Because you can expect to spend a minimum of eight to ten hours per day five or six days a week at your job, it is important to enjoy it. The most difficult job in the world is one you don't like. Therefore, for your career success – not to mention your mental health – find a work environment you will enjoy.

The Great Place to Work® Institute[7] offers some guidance about what to look for in a workplace. They say that trust between management

...ATTRIBUTE OF THE STRONG

and employee is key to a healthy workplace. A great place to work is one in which you "trust the people you work for, have pride in what you do, and enjoy the people you work with."

They also suggest that it is helpful to have the following five qualities present in the workplace:

1. **Credibility**
   - communication is open and accessible
   - there is competence in coordinating human and material resources
   - there is integrity in carrying out the company vision;

2. **Respect**
   - the company supports professional development and shows appreciation
   - the company collaborates with employees on relevant decisions
   - the company cares for employees as individuals and is aware of their personal lives;

3. **Fairness**
   - there is equity and balanced treatment for everyone in terms of rewards
   - there is impartiality and an absence of favoritism in hiring and promotions
   - there is justice, in the form of a lack of discrimination and a process for appeals;

4. **Pride**
   - in your personal job and in individual contributions
   - in the work produced by your team or work group
   - in the organization's products and standing in the community; and

5. **Camaraderie**
   - an opportunity to be oneself
   - a socially friendly and welcoming atmosphere
   - a sense of "family" or "team."

Whether you are the employer trying to create a healthy workplace, or the employee looking for an enjoyable place to work, make sure these qualities are present.

Because compensation plays a relatively minor role in overall job satisfaction, it is better to enjoy what you are doing and look forward to going to work every day than to take a job strictly for the money. If money is the only motivation, chances are you won't be happy for long.

164 Some things to remember when you want to appear confident around a boardroom table

WEDNESDAY

1. Sit up straight in your chair;
2. Deliver one sentence in one breath. Subtly take a deep breath before a long sentence so that you are forceful when you are speaking; and
3. When looking at the people around the table, look into their eyes. If you are uncomfortable doing this, look at the bridges of their noses.

165 A wise man has doubts even in his best moments. Real truth is always accompanied by hesitations

THURSDAY

— *Henry David Thoreau (1817–1862)*

Nothing is ever black or white. There is usually some grey area that you may not initially perceive. Understand that, while it is very important to have firm convictions about something, leave room for some doubt. It will keep you grounded and help you to be cautious.

TO LIVE

166 Treasure the love you receive above all. It will survive long after your gold and good health have vanished

— *Og Mandino (1923–1996)*

FRIDAY O₂

Understand that it is your loved ones who will support and care for you without any qualification. Money can hire doctors, nurses or attendants to look after you, but they will look after your physical body only. Loved ones look after more than this.

Given this reality, it makes perfect sense to spend more time nurturing your loved ones than nurturing your bank account. Keep in mind this truism: on their deathbed, no one ever says they wish they had spent more time at the office.

Whatever life path you take, never forget the importance of family.

167 It's often difficult to remember people's names when you are first introduced to them

SATURDAY

RPUN

Everyone like to be remembered, and therefore it's important to work at remembering names. Forgetting implies you don't think they're important. To help in remembering their name, **RPUN**:

Repeat their name to them while being introduced. For example, when introduced to Alan Maddox, immediately say "Alan, it is a pleasure to meet you."

Make a **P**icture out of their name and place that picture on the person's forehead. If you met Alan, picture an ox or bull that is very upset (a "mad ox") trying to connect a number of computers together (putting together **a l**ocal **a**rea **n**etwork). This method will take some practice and some creativity; however, it is a worthwhile exercise.

Use their name in the conversation if you continue to talk to them for an extended period. Not only will this help you remember their name, but it will also make the other person receptive to you, because everyone likes to hear his or her own name.

Finally, after the event is over, make Notes about the person you've met. You can do this on the back of their business card (if you have exchanged cards), in a separate card file or in an electronic organizer.

168 Fear knocked at the door. Faith answered. No one was there

SUNDAY

— Old English proverb

You can interpret this proverb two ways: as it applies to your faith in God, or to your faith in yourself. God will be there to help you if you ask. But even before you get to the point of asking for His help, you should believe you have the ability to overcome the challenges you face. Be strong. Have faith.

169 You Must Not Quit

MONDAY

When things go wrong, as they sometimes will,
    When the road you're trudging seems all uphill,
    When the funds are low and the debts are high,
    And you want to smile, but you have to sigh,
    When care is pressing you down a bit –
    Rest if you must, but don't you quit.

Life is queer with its twists and turns,
    As every one of us sometimes learns,
    And many a fellow turns about
    When he might have won had he stuck it out.
    Don't give up though the pace seems slow –
    You may succeed with another blow.

Often the goal is nearer than
　　It seems to a faint and faltering man;
　　Often the struggler has given up
　　When he might have captured the victor's cup;
　　And he learned too late when the night came down,
　　How close he was to the golden crown.
　　Success is failure turned inside out –
　　The silver tint in the clouds of doubt,
　　And you never can tell how close you are,
　　It might be near when it seems afar;
　　So stick to the fight when you're hardest hit –
　　It's when things seem worst that you must not quit.

　　— Author Unknown

Keep trying, no matter what the circumstances. Success is often closer than you think.

170　There will be times when you need to negotiate

It could be your starting salary at your new job, the purchase price of a new car, or a new labor contract with your employees.

There are four things to keep in mind if you want to be a successful negotiator. Together they make up a **PIPE**:

Person: make sure you separate the person from the issue or problem. Don't let your emotions enter into it;

Interests: determine the real interests of the person you are negotiating with. Don't focus on their stated position, but rather try to determine what is really important to them;

Prepared: be prepared going in. Have a credible reason for what you are asking for and be prepared to articulate it. As well, be prepared to be flexible and have one or more options ready that are equally attractive to you; and

Equal: try to work it so that both parties go away feeling they have won (or at least not lost).

Use this framework for any kind of negotiations, big or small. No matter the size, bring along a **PIPE**.

171 When writing a report or making a presentation, you need to know what kind of audience you are addressing

The type of audience will determine the structure of your presentation.

If you expect the audience to readily accept or be favorable toward your message, then the audience is known as a "receptive" audience. In contrast, if the audience is likely to require some convincing, it is classified as a "hostile" audience. You need to know which type you are addressing because it impacts how you structure your argument.

If your audience is hostile, it is important to build your case well before you state your conclusion. That is, discuss the background, the facts and the reasons before you present your conclusion. This way, you will have the opportunity to convince your audience of your viewpoint before they have to consider your conclusion.

If you have a receptive audience, state your case at the outset, and then present your reasons. If you did it the other way around, you run the risk of boring (and maybe even alienating) your friendly audience, because they already agree with you.

172 Never be ashamed to admit what you do not know

— *Arabic proverb*

If you are asked something and you do not know the answer, admit that you don't know. It is far better to confess lack of knowledge about something than to try to make up an answer. Someone around you may know the correct answer, and if you try to "fake it" you could end up looking very foolish.

173 The Boy, the Nails and the Fence

Grandpa Frank used to tell the story about one of his students who had a bad temper. As a way of trying to help him gain control over it, Grandpa gave the boy a bag of nails and told him that every time he lost his temper, he had to hammer a nail into the old fence out behind his house.

On the first day, the boy drove ten nails into the fence. Over the next few weeks, as he learned to control his anger, the number of nails hammered into the fence gradually dwindled. The boy discovered that it was easier to hold his temper than to walk all the way to the back fence and drive nails into it. Finally, the day came when the boy didn't lose his temper at all. He told Grandpa Frank about it – who was understandably pleased – but was then told to pull out one nail for each day that he was able to hold his temper.

Months passed and finally the boy was able to tell Grandpa Frank that all the nails were gone. Grandpa then took the boy and led him down to the fence.

They stood in front of it and Grandpa Frank said, "You've done well getting your temper under control, but look at all the holes in the fence. The fence will never be the same. When you say things in anger, they leave a scar just like on this fence. You can put a knife in a person and draw it out but it won't matter how many times you say 'I'm sorry,' the wound is still there."

— *Author Unknown*

Remember that a verbal wound can be as bad as, and even worse than, a physical one.

174 It's hard to be funny when you have to be clean

— Mae West (1893–1980)

If you can make someone laugh without resorting to off-color or dirty jokes, then you are legitimately funny. You can always get a laugh if you tell a dirty joke, because most people will guffaw or snicker at a sex-related joke, if for no other reason than to imply that they know what is being laughed about. If you do feel compelled to tell dirty jokes, understand that there is a time and place for them – never in mixed company and never as part of a speech to an audience.

Better yet is to develop a repertoire of good, clean jokes; this way, you will never offend anybody, regardless of the situation.

175 If you have not been trustworthy in handling worldly wealth, who will trust you with true riches

—Luke 16:11

Cultivate a good attitude about wealth. It's okay to be wealthy, but make sure you use your money wisely. Money can help make for a better life, but be sure it is not only your life you are bettering. In short, spread the wealth.

176 Yesterday is history, tomorrow is a mystery and today is a gift: that's why we call it the present

— Brian Dyson (b. 1936)

You cannot change your past. You have some control over your future because it is based on your actions today. But even so, events happen that will change your plans and take you in a completely different direction. Therefore, in reality the only time in your life that you have direct control over is today. Make sure you enjoy it. Tell your loves ones how you feel about them, celebrate the high mark you received

...AND OTHERS WILL RESPECT YOU

on the exam, or revel in your job promotion. Take pleasure in seeing those you care about reach milestones – you never know when it will happen again. Enjoy life now.

177 The 3:1 AtP Rule

When you are in a nurturing role, whether as a tutor, boss, mentor, leader or even parent, remember to practice the "3:1 AtP" rule.

To ensure people listen to you over the long haul, you need to employ the 3:1 AtP rule. This is particularly important when you have to provide advice or offer constructive criticism to people on an ongoing basis, e.g., subordinates or children. The premise of constructive criticism is to offer advice to help them better themselves. In order to communicate so that people accept what you have to say – and more importantly, act on it – you need to have said something positive to them beforehand. This is the "Accentuating the Positive" part. The ratio of positive to negative comments should be three to one.

The reason you need to have this three-to-one ratio of positive to negative is that it is critical to fostering the view that you say more positive things than negative; after all, most people view advice or criticism, constructive or not, as negative. If you aren't generally more positive in your comments than negative, people will come to expect that every time you approach them to say something, it will be negative. And because people don't like to hear negative things about themselves, they will be predisposed to "tune you out."

In virtually every environment – home, work, team – it is important to develop a culture in which people are receptive to your opinions. You do this by being known as someone who says more positive things than negative.

178 If you don't ask, you don't get

— Mahatma Gandhi (1869–1948)

Always ask for the order. Good salespeople always make sure they ask for the sale. Develop the mindset that it never hurts to ask for something. The worse that can happen (usually) is that the other person says "no."

This mindset means that you'll have to develop a thick skin and the ability to refrain from taking rejection personally. This is done by adopting the perspective that, when people say "no," they are saying it to the product or service you are selling and not to you as a person.

The key to successful selling is to be persistent without being pushy. Why is it important to have some sales ability? Because you are always selling something: a product, yourself for a job, your strategic vision as president of a company. If you need to convince anyone of anything – whether to buy your product, hire you, or accept your telephone calls – be determined, but don't be a pest. And always be willing to "ask for the order"; ask them to hire you, or to buy your product, or to give you an appointment. There are two possible outcomes when you ask: yes or no. If you get a yes, you got what you wanted. If no, well, you can't lose something that wasn't yours in the first place.

179 You should behave as you think is good, but not following the advice of the crowd

— Ralph Waldo Emerson (1803–1882)

You must control your moral compass and *you* must determine your moral direction. Figure out what the correct direction is and make sure the compass hand is always pointing the right way. Be prepared for some people to follow a direction that differs from yours. Don't follow their way; follow your own.

ALWAYS LAUGH

180 Pay yourself first

FRIDAY

Dave Chilton in The *Wealthy Barber*[8] says that an important factor to becoming wealthy is to learn to pay yourself first. He suggests that you have 10% of your pay deducted automatically from your paycheck for deposit into some kind of savings vehicle. This way, you will not see the money and therefore you won't miss it. Your lifestyle and spending habits will be based on the money you see (your take-home pay). If you don't have that 10% taken right off your paycheck you likely won't save, because most people's lifestyle expands to the size of their paycheck, whatever it may be.

Having money deducted directly from your paycheck is an effective method of saving because it is a forced investment plan. Making regular planned investments into a fund or a stock is called dollar-cost averaging. Dollar-cost averaging, where the investment is made on a regular basis regardless of the price, is a good technique that is part of a disciplined, systematic savings plan.

181 You cannot go to war on your butt

SATURDAY

War – working **a r**oom – should not be restricted to business events; it should also apply to social functions. Always take the opportunity to expand your network.

Whenever you are working a room, you need to be standing and moving around. The only exception to this rule is if your host has encouraged you to sit down. Otherwise you should not sit; you should mingle.

182 Going to church doesn't make you a Christian any more than going to a garage makes you a mechanic

— Author Unknown

Don't do anything partway. If you are going to do something, give it 100% effort. Going through the motions is a waste of your time and energy. This is particularly true as it pertains to your belief in God. Don't simply go through the motions; you may be able to fool the people in the congregation, but you will not fool God.

183 No one conquers who does not fight

— Gabriel Biel (c. 1420–1495)

If you expect to be successful in life, you need to be prepared to face challenges. In most cases, that will require you to move out of your "comfort zone." For example, you may have to leave your high school friends to go off to university; you may have to move away from your hometown to take a new job; or you may have to quit secure employment in order to be entrepreneurial. Understand that you cannot "win" without facing challenges. In life, unlike in the dictionary, "adversity" comes before "achievement."

184 A leader is anyone who has two characteristics: first, they are going someplace; second, they are able to persuade others to go with them

— W.H. Cowley

A leader needs to begin with a plan and then be able to articulate that plan with enough passion and enthusiasm that others will commit to it. Whenever you are in a leadership position, make sure you have a well-defined, well thought-out course of action. That's the first part. The second part, and the harder one, is getting others to commit to your plan. Motivating people is challenging and takes work. You can learn from others by watching how they get their message across and trying to emulate them. However, since the best teacher is experience itself, you must seek out situations in which you can be a leader and motivate people. Like many other things, leadership abilities improve with use.

185 Be nice to people on the way up because you will meet them on the way down

— *Corporate proverb*

If you have a healthy work ethic, an ability to work with people and some smarts, you will move up the corporate ladder. Remember, though, that no matter where you are in the corporate hierarchy, you need to treat everyone with respect. Keep this in mind for two reasons: first of all, chances are good that many of your peers will advance right alongside you, and you will need allies in your climb; second, it is unlikely your climb to the top will occur without some valleys. Some may take you down to levels below that of a few of the people you passed on your way up. If you mistreated them during your climb, you can expect to be treated the same way by them during your slide back down. This is the nature of the corporate world.

Understand that no one's career path is a straight line to the top. Make allies on your ascent so that you will have allies on any descent.

186 During the day you should behave in such a way that you can sleep at night in peace; and in your youth behave in such a way that you can live your old age in peace

— *Indian proverb*

Scandals or misdeeds from the past usually have a way of coming back to haunt people – it is rare someone can hide from them for an entire lifetime. Live such that you can grow old without worrying about keeping skeletons hidden away. You will lose enough sleep just dealing with the challenges of everyday life.

This attitude should be a constant in your life. Even though you will experience temptation, challenges and stressful situations along the road, adopt the mindset that you will never do anything unethical to get you out of a difficult situation.

187 Think like a turtle on a fence post

When you reach a goal, always remember to think of yourself as a turtle sitting on top of a fence post. Understand that you did not get there by yourself. Someone had to help you. Make sure you do something to reward others for helping you.

A turtle might use its fence post vantage point to survey the terrain ahead. But realize that the turtle needs others to help it get down and continue the journey. We all need others' help in life.

188 I'm done

When you want to show your host or waiter that you are finished eating, place your knife and fork at the two o'clock position, with the fork tines and knife blade together in the centre of the plate.

When finished eating, place your napkin loosely to the left of your plate on the table. Don't crumple or twist it up, as this shows nervousness; and don't fold it up nicely, as this may give the impression you think the host should re-use it without washing it. You should keep your napkin on your lap until everyone else is done eating and drinking. If others are not finished eating, keep the napkin on your lap.

189 The Serenity Prayer

SUNDAY

O God, grant me the serenity to accept the things I cannot change, the courage to change the things I can, and the wisdom to know the difference.

Living one day at a time, enjoying one minute at a time. Accepting hardships as the pathway to peace. Taking, as He did, this sinful world as it is, not as I would have it. Trusting that He will make all things right if I surrender to His will; that I may be reasonably happy in this life, and supremely happy with Him forever.

— *Reinhold Niebuhr (1892–1971)*

190 Strive to turn a weakness into a strength

MONDAY

There is a story of a ten-year-old boy who took up judo despite the fact that he had lost his left arm in a car accident.

The boy was taught by an old Japanese judo master and proved to be an avid student with a great attitude. Despite his early success, the boy wondered why it was that after one year of training that the teacher had taught him only one move.

"Sensei," the boy finally said, "shouldn't I be learning more moves?"

"This is the only move you'll ever need to know," the Sensei replied.

Not quite understanding, but believing in his Sensei, the boy kept training.

Several months later, seeing his progress, the Sensei entered the boy in his first tournament. Surprising everybody, including himself, the boy won his first two matches, primarily because of sheer determination and effort. The third match proved more difficult. After some time and much feinting back and forth, the boy's opponent became impatient and charged, but the boy deftly used his one and only move to win the match. Amazingly, this win put him into the finals.

His opponent in the final was bigger, stronger and more experienced than any other competitor he had met. From the outset, the one-armed boy appeared to be overmatched. Concerned that he might get hurt, the referee called a timeout to discuss with the judges whether to stop the match; the Sensei intervened. "No," the Sensei insisted.

The match resumed and very quickly his opponent made a critical mistake: he dropped his guard, and the boy instantly used his one and only move to pin him. Despite having no left arm, the boy won the match and the tournament. He was the champion!

On the way home, the boy and the Sensei reviewed each match in detail. Then the boy summoned the courage to ask what was really on his mind.

"Sensei, how did I win the tournament with only one move?"

"You won for two reasons," the Sensei answered. "First, through months of diligent practice, you've mastered one of the most difficult throws in all of judo.

"And second, the only known defense for that move is for your opponent to grab your left arm."

The boy's biggest weakness was in fact his greatest strength.

— *Author Unknown*

Identify your weaknesses. You may need to ask someone to help you, because typically people are not good at seeing their own weaknesses. Once you find out, challenge yourself to find a way to use them to your advantage.

191 Teach them

When you need to deliver a speech or presentation in which you must teach the audience something or convey a lot of information, use the **t³** method.

...YOU KNOW MORE THAN YOU THINK YOU DO

Begin your presentation by telling the audience what you are going to **tell** them, **tell** them, and then **tell** them what you told them. This repetition will help the audience remember your message.

t^3 should be done within the structure of the following outline:

1. **Opening**
   a) capture the audience's attention by beginning with a joke or a fact that will get their attention
   b) then tell them the topic of your presentation (t^1);
2. **Body**
   a) first point
      i. tell them the fact (t^2)
      ii. provide supporting material for the fact or statement;
   b) second point (if there is one)
      i. tell them the fact
      ii. provide supporting material for the fact or statement; and
3. **Conclusion**
   a) review or summarize what you have just told them (t^3)
   b) close strongly, either by challenging the audience to take some kind of action or delivering a memorable statement.

192 He liked people; therefore people liked him

— Mark Twain (1835–1910)

If you show enthusiasm, warmth and respect toward your colleagues, they will generally show you the same in return. But make sure you are sincere about it; an act will be seen through.

193 We often take for granted the very things that most deserve our gratitude

— Cynthia Ozick (b. 1928)

Or, as Joni Mitchell (b. 1943) sang, "You don't know what you've got 'til it's gone." This is particularly apropos when it comes to speaking about families. Don't take your family for granted. Treat siblings with respect and elders with reverence.

Other things you should appreciate are your health, your freedom, your right to vote, the shelter over your head, and your ability to worship your God freely. If you are ever in doubt about the importance of these things, ask a person who is dying what their biggest wish would be; or ask a homeless person in the middle of winter what they would most like at that moment; or ask a person who has been punished for his religious beliefs.

Make sure you regularly examine the good things you have in your life, and be thankful for them. If you have difficulty coming up with things to be thankful for, picture yourself without some of those things. If that picture is not a happy one, then they are things you should value.

194 Once you acquire a luxury, it quickly becomes a necessity. Wants easily become needs

Be careful about accumulating too many "luxuries" too soon. A luxury is something that is non-essential but that gives pleasure and comfort.

Your financial situation will fluctuate over the course of your life. Life circumstances will change: children are born, you go back to school, you take a pay cut at work, or you lose your job. During those times, certain previously enjoyed luxuries may be too expensive. You need to appreciate that the disappointment you experience when you have to give something up is far more intense than the pleasure you enjoyed when you first got it (and that pleasure was in the past, so it doesn't do anything for you now). Therefore, be slow in accumulating luxuries when you are young. Once you have them, luxuries tend to become needs – and it is very difficult to give up needs.

Horace (65 BC–8 BC) said, "He is almost always a slave who cannot live on a little." Don't become a slave.

LAUGHTER IS

195 Handwritten notes

SATURDAY

Emails, voice mails and text messages have made our world an increasingly impersonal one. If someone gives you a gift or does something nice for you, make an effort to send them a handwritten thank-you note. A handwritten note cuts through today's electronic clutter and will be remembered by the recipient.

196 To vanquish sin, you must accept that the root of each sin is in a bad thought. We are all only consequences of what we think

SUNDAY

— *Buddha (c. 563 BC–c. 483 BC)*

Is it possible to go through life without sinning? No.

Is it possible to go through life trying not to sin? Of course, but it requires dedication.

Because we are not perfect, we will sin despite our best intentions. One hopes those sins will be little ones; being envious of your neighbor's new car, for instance, is human nature; uttering the odd profanity. The big ones, such as murder, adultery and stealing, require a conscious, concerted effort and therefore cannot be justified under any circumstances.

In order to avoid an escalation of sinful activities, you must avoid putting yourself in a position where serious sins are seen as acceptable. Choose your friends and acquaintances wisely. If you consort with people who believe that recreational drugs are acceptable, or that cheating on schoolwork doesn't hurt anybody, then you will tend to think the same way.

If in your mind you can justify small transgressions, understand that you have to be very careful. With that kind of attitude, it is very easy to become able to justify big ones. The best advice: if you know something is wrong, don't do it, no matter how small it seems.

To paraphrase what Buddha is saying above: "We are shaped by our thoughts. We become what we think." Therefore, in your mind you need to have the proper image of yourself, your actions and your path. Picture yourself as successful and ethical... and you will be.

197 Courage is resistance to fear, mastery of fear, not absence of fear

MONDAY

— *Mark Twain (1835–1910)*

The word "courage" will have different meanings during the different stages in your life.

In first grade, courage was needed when you had to be left alone at school on that first day. In high school, it was when you had to stand up to the bully. Later in life, it may be when you have to confront a life-threatening disease.

Courage and fear are inseparable; they are two sides of the same coin. You cannot show courage without also facing fear. Know that each time you confront your fears, no matter how trivial they may seem, you exemplify courage... regardless of the outcome.

198 It is better to have a horrible end than horror without end

TUESDAY

— *German proverb*

If you are in an unpleasant situation, it is better to end it right away – even if ending it will result in a horrible scene – than to continue to suffer over the long-term.

Some examples might be when you have to fire an underperforming employee, quit working for a boss who mistreats you, or when you have to break off a difficult relationship or friendship. Make the tough decision and end it. It may be painful now, but it will make your life (and theirs) easier going forward.

TWO PEOPLE

...BETWEEN

199 The truth is always the strongest argument

— Sophocles (c. 496 BC–406 BC)

Not only is it easier to remember facts or stories if they are true, it is also easier to defend your position if it is based on truth. If something is true, you are able to speak with the conviction that you cannot be contradicted. You can have differences of opinion or differing viewpoints about a situation, but if you know you are speaking from a position of truth, no one can accurately refute what you are saying.

200 Success

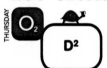

Your success at university or at work starts with your **d²**: your **d**esire to learn; and your **d**iscipline – how focused you are.

No doubt there will be distractions when you start something new: like the social life/new friends at university; or the extra pocket money and the new "toys" you can afford with a regular paycheck. But be sure to manage the distractions appropriately. Remember: **D²**.

201 I'm depressed

Be aware of signs of depression in yourself or your loved ones. Signs of mild depression include continued exhaustion, disinterest and distractedness. Mild depression can escalate into something more severe and lead to performance problems at work or school. It can even lead to life-altering events.

Depression is thought by some healthcare practitioners to be the result of anger turned inward. If you see signs of depression in yourself or your loved ones, try to determine the cause of it. Do whatever you can to release the anger and turn it outward; don't internalize it. Find a positive outlet so you can get the anger out into the open to be dealt with effectively.

202 How to make small talk

SATURDAY

The ability to make "small talk" is an acquired skill. Small talk needs to come across as natural and pleasant, and the way to get good at it is to practise it as much as possible.

One effective way to initiate small talk is to ask a question. This gets the other person talking. As well, asking a question implies that you are interested in what the other person has to say. Here are some examples of easy introductory questions: Did you enjoy the food? What do you think of the house/room/facility? Do you know the bride/groom? How do you think the [pick a subject, e.g., the local sports team] is doing?

Small talk should serve as an icebreaker to get the conversation going or fill in any awkward silences. Potentially emotional topics such as politics or religion should be avoided.

203 The Ten Commandments

SUNDAY

The Ten Commandments provide guidelines for living a good life. Follow them as closely as you can – especially the fifth one!

1. You shall have no other gods before me.
2. You shall not make yourselves an idol.
3. You shall not misuse the name of the Lord your God.
4. Remember the Sabbath by keeping it holy.
5. Honor your father and your mother.
6. You shall not commit murder.
7. You shall not commit adultery.
8. You shall not steal.
9. You shall not give false testimony against your neighbor.
10. You shall not covet.

— Exodus 20:2-17 and Deuteronomy 5:6-21

LIFE ITSELF

204 Keep your face to the sunshine and you cannot see the shadow

MONDAY

— Helen Keller (1880–1968)

If you consistently look on the bright side – striving to find the positive things in life – the negatives won't get you down so much.

Become known for having a "sunny" disposition. It will help you to be popular with friends and colleagues, and will help you fight the negativity that tries to creep up on us. Think of negativity as a shadow, and positivity as the light. Remember: the brighter the light, the weaker the shadow.

205 Yikes! A Job Interview

TUESDAY

There are three very important rules to keep in mind when you go to a job interview:

1. Be on time;
2. Be well-dressed; and
3. Be prepared.

When having an interview, you should be prepared for some "stress" or "off-the-wall" questions, in addition to the standard ones about your background. Stress questions are asked for two reasons: one, to gauge how well you handle unexpected events; and two, to get you out of the pre-programmed interview answers. When you do get these types of questions, be calm and don't rush to answer. If you need to buy some time to collect your thoughts, ask for clarification.

Some examples of those questions might be: "How would you improve the design of the hockey stick?" or "What is your favorite planet?"

Interviewers have even been known to ask you what kind of animal you would describe yourself as. It is a seemingly silly question, but one whose answer can actually say much about a person.

A response might be that you are a lion – king of the jungle – but this is not a very creative one (and one that many people would probably give). Another possible answer might be that you are like a hyena, because it is an efficient hunter that works best in groups and has a sense of humor.

One answer that may separate you from everybody else is that you are like a turtle. Remember that the turtle started slowly against a faster opponent but still ended up winning the race (showing both an ability to overcome big odds and a history of success); it is one of the longest-living creatures in the animal kingdom (showing longevity); it has a hard outer shell (a thick skin); and in order to get ahead, it has to stick its neck out (therefore, it is not risk-averse).

206 I will speak ill of no man, and speak all the good I know of everybody

WEDNESDAY

— *Benjamin Franklin (1706–1790)*

In addition to being one of the founding fathers of the United States, Ben Franklin was also a scientist (experimented with electricity), an inventor (bifocal glasses), a businessman (he set up a fire insurance company), a musician (he played the violin, harp and guitar), and a printer (his initial training). He was a busy guy.

Of all of his many talents, however, statesmanship may have been his greatest. Among other things, he was one of the signatories to the U.S. Declaration of Independence and the U.S. Constitution. His ability to get people to work toward a common goal – the formation of a nation – was exceptional. One of the skills he employed to do this was by being generous in his praise of people, and stingy with criticism or gossip. Try to follow his example.

207 Stay in School

THURSDAY

It is very important that you continue your education through your young adult life. The ages from 18–30 should be spent getting the best education possible in order to set the foundation for the next 40 years of your working life (yes, that means working until you are 70!). The years 18–24 should be spent in full-time studies: college, university or apprenticing. Ages 24–30 should be spent at a job or jobs in which you experience a broad cross-section of activities. You'll find that, after about age 30, the time you will need to devote to your family responsibilities (spouse and children) will increase, crowding out the time for formal education. Therefore, it is vital to finish the formal part of your education before your family requires your presence on an ongoing and regular basis.

Formal education should give you three things:
1. The technical knowledge required to do a job;
2. The ability to communicate effectively (in particular an ability to write well); and
3. Assistance in making you a well-rounded individual.

Being able to write well is very important because the ability to communicate effectively is a foundation of a successful career. Therefore, regardless of the educational pursuit you choose, make sure you learn to write effectively. You need to appreciate that, despite your being a very bright person, others may not see this if you cannot effectively convey your thoughts in writing.

Being well-read is important because it helps you to be conversant and comfortable in any situation. And the more situations in which you feel comfortable, the more opportunities you will have to broaden your business and social network. Becoming well-read means reading up on a breadth of subjects. Your sources can be books on science, magazine articles on economics, newspaper editorials on politics, or blogs on developments in the Middle East. It may mean taking Greek literature courses at university in addition to your law studies, or it may mean taking night courses on twentieth-century history while apprenticing for your journeyman ticket.

In summary, take advantage of your young-adult years to get your education. It's much more difficult to do so during the family years.

208 Home ownership

A rule of thumb is that the expenses associated with home ownership – mortgage, utilities and taxes – should be no more than your 35% of your after-tax income. Be very careful not to buy a house whose all-in costs (those three items collectively) are too high for your household income. By the time you first deduct 10% of your paycheck for savings (see Day 180) and 35% for mortgage payments, you will have only 55% of your paycheck left for food, car expenses, clothing, household expenses, kids' activities and anything else.

When buying a house or condo, it is often easy to be enticed into spending more than you can afford. This can occur by way of paying a higher price than you had budgeted, or it may be by taking on a mortgage of a longer duration than you had planned (causing you to pay more interest over the life of the mortgage). When you buy a house, make sure you consider what the next five to ten years of your life have in store for you in terms of earnings. For example, if you are a two-income household when you buy the house, but planning on having children and hoping for one parent to stay at home with the kids, make sure you take into consideration the loss of that second income.

We all hope our paycheck will increase over the years, but we all need to consider the ramifications if it doesn't.

209 Shaking Hands

When shaking hands, your grip should be firm but not too hard. Look the other person in the eye and make sure you are smiling as you shake their hand. When you meet someone for the first time, there should be no more than two up-and-down motions. You can shake hands for a longer period if you know the person. Some people cup their left hand over the other person's right hand, but don't do this unless you know the person very well.

SUCCESS

210

SUNDAY

The commandments of God should be followed because of love of God, not because of fear of God

— The Talmud

There are basic rules of conduct we need to follow to ensure "order" in our society. The understanding that there will be penalties for breaking those rules is fundamental to maintaining social stability. Those basic rules of conduct were given to us thousands of years ago by God.

Our motivation to follow God's rules should be based on the understanding that they are in our best interests and are good for us. Adopt the attitude that the rules given by God – such as the Ten Commandments (see last Sunday, Day 203) – have been given to us by a loving God. Accept and follow His rules with the attitude that they are good for us, rather than having the attitude that we will be punished if we don't follow them. The difference between the two attitudes is this: it is easier to stay the course when we take a positive attitude toward something; it is harder to stay motivated when we have a negative one.

211

MONDAY

To win without risk is to triumph without glory

— Pierre Corneille (1606–1684)

Why do so many lottery winners end up unhappy? Because the money was given to them; they did not earn it. Why do so many children of rich families suffer from "affluenza," i.e., not succeeding when they have been given every opportunity to do so? Because things were given to them – they didn't have to work for them.

In order to "win" – that is, achieve what you set out to do – you must work for it. Otherwise, the victory is hollow and short-lived. If you have earned your success because of your hard work and determination, it will be something you can legitimately be proud of, and the feeling of accomplishment will be intense and long-lasting.

212 He who has no fire in himself cannot warm others

PEE

— Author Unknown

If you need to get people fired up and ready to go, you must show your **pee**. That is, you must exude **p**assion, **e**nthusiasm and **e**xcitement.

213 First impressions are very important

Here are some hints to help you make a good first impression when you speak to a group of people (large or small).

The most critical part of the meeting or presentation is the first minute. People will make judgments based on those first few seconds.

In the case of a speech or presentation, once you are introduced, walk purposely and confidently to the speaking position. If there is no introduction, or if it is an informal or impromptu gathering, stand tall and try to make an immediate connection with the audience by establishing eye contact. Smile warmly.

If you are speaking to a large group of people, it is a good idea to try to mingle with the audience before you speak. Move around and get comfortable with some audience members ahead of time. This will help put you more at ease when you are standing in front of them. When it is time for you to begin your speech, take a deep breath just prior to beginning. This does two things: helps you to relax; and helps you to start speaking in a clear, loud voice.

One final thing to remember is that you as the speaker should be at least as well dressed as the best-dressed person in the group or audience. It is important to show your respect for the audience by dressing up for them.

...TO FOLLOW THROUGH

214 Give a man a fish and you feed him for a day. Teach a man to fish and you feed him for a lifetime

THURSDAY O₂

— Chinese proverb

It is tempting to try to do everything yourself rather than teaching someone else, especially when you are pressed for time. Whether it is preparing Christmas dinner, putting together presentations at work, or looking after the family finances, it is often easier and faster to do it yourself (at least initially). However, understand that the extra time you take now to teach someone to do something will save you time in the future. Taking the time to teach others helps both of you: you, because it will free up your time to do other things; and them, because you will help them to develop a skill. By being a teacher rather than a doer, you help two people.

215 The Jar

FRIDAY O₂

One day Grandpa Frank brought a four-litre, wide-mouthed jar to class and set it on the table in front of him. He told the class that the jar represented their life, and the inside of the jar represented the time they had to enjoy it.

He began the demonstration by grabbing about a dozen fist-sized rocks and carefully placing them, one at a time, into the jar. When the jar was filled to the top and no more rocks could fit inside, he asked, "Is this jar full?"

Everyone in the class agreed that it was. He responded, "Really?"

He reached under the table and pulled out a bucket of gravel. He dumped some of the gravel in and shook the jar, causing pieces of gravel to work themselves down into the spaces between the big rocks. Then he asked the group once more, "Is the jar full?"

This time the class was on to him. "Probably not," one answered.

"Good!" he replied. Grandpa Frank reached under the table and brought out a bucket of sand. He started to dump the sand in and it went into all of the spaces left between the rocks and the gravel. Once more he asked the question, "Is the jar full?"

"No!" the class shouted. Once again he said, "Good!" Then he grabbed a bottle of wine and poured it in until the jar was filled to the brim. He looked up at the class and asked, "Okay now, there are two points made in this illustration. What are they?"

One eager student raised his hand and said, "One is that no matter how full your schedule is, if you try really hard you can always fit some more things into it!"

"No," Grandpa Frank replied. "Although people often think that about their life, that's not one of them."

He went on to say, "This exercise teaches us two things: first, if you don't put the big rocks in first, you'll never get them in at all. The big rocks are the important things in your life – things like spending time with your loved ones, looking after your health, practising your faith, furthering your education, and looking after your financial well-being. You must put the big rocks in first or you will never get them in at all."

"The second thing is that, no matter how full your schedule is, there is always room for a little bit of pleasure."

— *Author Unknown*

Samuel Smiles (1812–1904) said: "The secret of happiness is to enjoy small pleasures."

The activities and challenges of daily life tend to expand to fill hours in a day. Make a point of carving out time to enjoy.

216 How to use a knife and fork

The proper technique for using a fork and knife is as follows:
1. Hold the fork in your left hand and the knife in your right;

2. Hold the knife and fork at each end and place your index finger along the top of each utensil (do not hold them like a dagger!);
3. Face the tines downward and hold down an end-piece of whatever you are cutting; and
4. Using a gentle sawing motion, cut your food near the tines of the fork so that you have one bite-sized piece.

In North America, it is common practice to place your knife down onto your plate, switch the fork to your right hand, and then bring your food to your mouth. In Europe, it is common practice to keep your fork in your left hand.

217 When you are so afraid that your knees knock, kneel on them

SUNDAY

— Author Unknown

Prayer can be very helpful during difficult times in your life. Whether it is facing a life-threatening illness, speaking to an audience, or writing the entrance exam for medical school, prayer provides comfort. Keep in mind that God does answer knee mail.

When your prayers do get answered, remember it. Always give thanks when the power of prayer helps you through challenging times.

218 I can complain that the rose bush has thorns, or I can rejoice that the thorn bush has roses

MONDAY

— Jean-Baptiste Alphonse Karr (1808–1890)

Challenge yourself to find the positive side of a negative situation. If you reflect on the situation closely enough, you should be able to find something positive in it. By taking away something positive, you've turned a bad thing into something good.

219 Do good to thy friend to keep him, to thy enemy to gain him

TUESDAY

— Ben Franklin (1706–1790)

It will be highly unlikely you will go through life without making an enemy or two, or at the very least having someone not like you very much. Sometimes the reason for the animosity will be justified, and sometimes not. Whether in your business or your personal life, you don't want to have too many enemies. On the contrary, you want to surround yourself with people who will help you succeed. Therefore, if you do something to upset someone, try to make amends by doing something positive for them. They will usually be impressed by your maturity and professionalism.

However, if you are not able to turn an enemy into a friend, remember to "keep your friends close and your enemies closer". You need to be aware of what your enemies are doing. It is important, because they don't have your best interests at heart and may be consciously or unconsciously trying to impede your progress. Therefore, keep them close to you so that you can keep an eye on them.

220 A strong leader needs to be fanatical

WEDNESDAY

When you are a leader in an organization that has more than two or three layers of personnel, you must be fanatical about communicating your message. That message could pertain to the quality of the company's product, to the work ethic you expect, to the moral guidelines you want followed, or to the key factors necessary for your organization's success. You need to be fanatical because of the "dilution factor." The more layers there are in the organization, the more diluted your message will be by the time it reaches the bottom layer. That is, as it gets relayed down through the levels of the organization, it will lose more and more of its intensity.

The definition of a fanatic is "a person whose strong admiration for something is considered to be extreme or unreasonable." In order to

WILL APPEAR

...THE TEACHER

make sure your message is received and understood by even the most junior person in your company, you need to be a fanatic – in other words, border on the "extremely unreasonable."

221 Money is like drinking saltwater, the more you drink, the thirstier you get

— *Roman proverb*

There is nothing wrong with money. Capitalism, one of the most important societal developments of the last 1,000 years because it increased the standard of living in all places where it was practiced freely, is based on the pursuit of money. Yet, while the pursuit of money can be a good thing, the attitude that you continually need more is not. At some point in your life you must determine when the drive to accumulate more money, wealth or material goods has to take a back seat to the more important things in your life, e.g., your responsibilities to, and relationships with, your family, friends and loved ones. This realization will likely mean you have to make some changes in your life. This might include working fewer hours, driving a less expensive car, or giving up a fancy annual vacation. There will be a time in your life when nurturing the really important investments in your life – marriage, children, charitable work – must take precedence over your financial investments. Don't let that point in time happen too late in your life.

222 The Starfish

One day Uncle Craig saw Grandpa Frank standing at the beach facing the ocean. The tide had washed ashore hundreds of starfish and they were beginning to die of exposure. Grandpa Frank was standing there methodically tossing the starfish back into the ocean one at a time in a slow, meditative series of motions.

Seeing the sheer number of the starfish dying on the beach, Uncle Craig said to Grandpa Frank, "Why do you even bother? It won't make any difference."

Grandpa Frank stopped for a moment, looked at the starfish in his hand and replied, "It will to this one."

— *Author Unknown*

You have the power to make a difference in someone's life. Make the effort.

223 Excuse me... I'd like to say something

There may be times when you would like to break into a conversation at work or a party. If you do, remember to "include, don't intrude." Do not approach two people who are deeply involved in a conversation. It is better to approach a group of three or more. When you approach the group, begin by positioning yourself nearby. Once there, begin by giving facial feedback – smiling, laughing or making eye contact. Don't start talking immediately; once you receive verbal acknowledgement from a group member or you receive eye contact and a smile, then you can join in.

224 He who walks in integrity walks securely

— *Proverbs 10:9*

Generally speaking, you will find that people who are honest and forth-right are confident individuals. They tend to have a healthy self-esteem and often project a sense of calmness about them. This "presence" evolves because they are comfortable with their actions and have nothing to be ashamed of.

225 Persistence

MONDAY

Calvin Coolidge (1872–1933) said:

"Nothing in the world can take the place of persistence.
Talent will not; nothing is more common than unsuccessful men with talent.
Genius will not; unrewarded genius is almost a proverb.
Education will not; the world is full of educated derelicts.
Persistence and determination alone are omnipotent."

A synonym for omnipotent is unstoppable. Substitute it in the last line and it reads: Persistence and determination alone are unstoppable.

226 Loose lips sink ships

TUESDAY

— from World War II posters

During the Second World War, instructions were given to the soldiers that they were not to talk about any aspect of the war when writing letters to home. The concern was that the enemy could intercept the letters, or that their loved ones could inadvertently and unknowingly disclose sensitive information to someone who could pass the information to the enemy.

This same principle applies in business as well. The less you say about your business, the better. Never say anything about your company's strategic plans or business capabilities unless instructed to do so by your superiors. The less your competitors know about you and your business, the better off you are.

P.S. "Loose lips sink ships" applies to your personal life as well. Don't tell secrets. It could sink a friendship.

227 A successful organization

To have a successful company, or even a department within an organization, you must have good people working for you. They have to share your values, goals and work ethic.

Consider that no matter how good the chef is, no collection of rotten eggs will produce a good-tasting omelet. Make sure you have the right kind people working for you. If you don't, make changes.

228 Before you get pregnant

Females in their childbearing years need to be aware of the importance of a good diet and to practice it even before they get pregnant. Studies have found that roughly half of all pregnancies are unplanned[9]. Therefore, don't wait to start practising good dietary habits until you are pregnant, because you just might get a little surprise.

What are good dietary practices? The food pyramid is a good start (see Day 39); but it also includes moderate alcohol consumption and no smoking. If you suspect you are pregnant, do not drink **any** alcohol – alcohol consumption can cause Fetal Alcohol Syndrome (FAS) in the newborn. It is also important to maintain a healthy weight and to have a diet that is rich in essential micronutrients, especially folic acid, vitamin D and vitamin A, which are all particularly good for a baby's healthy development. There is a lot of information available on eating right. Find it and read it.

229 In the end it's not the years in your life that count. It's the life in your years

— *Abraham Lincoln (1809–1865)*

Nobody knows how much time they have on earth. Enjoy each day as much as you can. Plan for the future, but enjoy today. If you want to skydive, go ahead and try it. If you want to swim with dolphins, do it. Don't put it off.

You need to live your life such that you can stop and reflect at any time and be pleased with where you are. Whether it applies to your relationships with your loved ones, your efforts at the office, your charity work, or your personal goals and achievements, you need to consider where you are every once in a while. If, upon reflection, you can say you are satisfied, then you are leading a good life.

230 Party On!

When you are at a social function and are working the room, keep moving around. Avoid speaking to one group of people or one person the entire time. You want to speak to as many people as possible in order to expand your network. Now, in order to be able to do this, you will have to make a graceful exit from a conversation at some point. Here is some guidance on how to do it:

Only exit a conversation after *you* have finished talking. Say, "Excuse me, it was interesting/nice talking to you." Then, offer an explanation such as, "I see someone I should also say hello to" or "I should go freshen up."

Then you need to physically go to a different area of the room or go do what you said you were going to do.

One word of caution: avoid looking like a "bumblebee." That is, don't flit from conversation to conversation. Make sure you spend enough time so that you become engaged with the people you talk to or meet.

231 Reputation is what men and women think of us; character is what God knows of us

— Thomas Paine (1737–1809)

Do everything possible to make sure your reputation is a good one. The foundation of a good reputation is good character. If you conduct yourself in a way you think would please God, then a good reputation will result.

232 The harder you work the harder it is to surrender

— Vince Lombardi (1913–1970)

If you work extremely hard at something, it becomes inherently difficult to give up on it. It's probably because of the time and energy you have put into it. If you give up, it's like you're cheating yourself. And nobody likes a cheater.

If you want to achieve something worthwhile, you have to commit to working hard to accomplish it. By making a commitment, and then by putting forth the sustained effort, thoughts of quitting will be crowded out of your mind because you are too busy working hard to think of anything else.

233 Lead On!

When you need to lead a group of people in completing a task, be aware of the 3 fs: frustration, fatigue and failure.

Be aware that frustration can lead to fatigue which can lead to failure. Do whatever you can to overcome any frustration that creeps into the group; if you don't, fatigue will inevitably set in. And once people get tired or worn out, it is hard to get them excited again. Try to head off the fatigue before it happens. If you notice people getting frustrated, stop for a while and try something new. Come back later when people are refreshed.

234 Always finish what you start

You must be disciplined enough to finish whatever job you start. Never leave something partway done. If you make it a habit of doing half a job, expect to get half a reputation.

235 It is smart to pick your friends – but not to pieces

— Author Unknown

One of the many jobs of parents is to know who their kids are hanging out with and to make sure those kids are a good influence. Beginning from when children are toddlers right up through the hormonally-charged teen years, parents need to try to make sure their kids have the "right" kinds of friends. After high school, however, parents have less control (if any) over the choice of friends.

Therefore, once you leave home, it is your responsibility to choose the right types of friends. Find people who share your values, are fun to be with, and will look out for your best interests.

Once you have found those people, accept your friends as they are, warts and all. Don't be critical of them. If you are, you may not have them as friends for long.

236 There is no pillow so soft as a clear conscience

— French proverb

Life is stressful enough with meeting work or school deadlines, raising kids, paying bills and writing exams. Don't add another level of stress by doing things you know are wrong. You will lose enough sleep dealing with the stresses of everyday life; you don't need to lose more worrying about getting "caught."

237 When to use your fingers

When you are served an entrée and you need to use your fingers (e.g., ribs or lobster), finger bowls will likely be provided. Usually there is a slice of lemon floating in the water. If you need to use the finger bowl to clean your fingers, delicately dip your fingertips in the water, dry them off with your napkin, and then set the bowl off to the side of your plate when you are finished.

238 The Cross Room

A young guy was pretty stressed out from the challenges of daily life and felt he was at the end of his rope. Seeing no way out, he dropped to his knees in prayer and said, "Lord, I can't go on. I have too heavy a cross to bear."

All of a sudden, there was a flash of light and the Lord appeared to him. "My son, if you can't bear the weight, bring your cross and come with me."

The two walked together in silence for a while and soon approached a huge building with two doors.

"Put your cross in the room through the door on the left. Then when you come out open the other door, go in, and pick any cross you like."

The young man was filled with relief. "Thank you, Lord."

After depositing his cross through the door on the left, he came back out and went through the second door, whereupon he saw hundreds of crosses. Some were so large they could barely fit inside the three-storey building. After some time, he finally spotted a tiny little cross leaning up against the far wall.

...THAN HE WHO THINKS HIMSELF SO

"I'd like that one, Lord."

"My son," the Lord replied, "that's the one you brought in."

– Author Unknown

Understand that everyone has challenges and problems. Every single one of us has a cross to bear, and some have more than one. Your burden may seem very heavy at times. However, no matter how heavy you think your cross is, don't yearn to change places with others. For all you know, their cross just may be heavier. Be satisfied with your life. Fight the battles and approach challenges with confidence. By doing so, you become stronger, and will soon find that your cross is not really that heavy after all.

239 That which does not kill you will only make you stronger

— Friedrich Nietzsche (1844–1900)

When you are faced with a very difficult situation or an unpleasant task – and expect to face those situations on more than a few occasions throughout your life – approach it with the mindset that you are going to become stronger because of it.

This attitude will not make the situation any more pleasant, but at least you know you will grow as a person as a result of having to go through it.

240 I'm new here

Entering a new environment (new city, new school, new job) can be difficult. Often you don't know anyone, and are unfamiliar with how things are normally done. One way to help your transition is to identify the **COIs** – the Centers of Influence – and try to get to know them.

A **COI** is not necessarily the boss, but rather someone who is held in high regard in the organization or the area. In the case of the workplace, it could be a long-time employee or the boss's secretary. In a university, it may be a professor, the student union rep, or a graduate student. In a new city, it may be a church minister, a school principal, or the owner of the local coffee shop.

What **COI**s all have in common is that they have the respect of the community. They may not necessarily be an actual elected leader, such as the mayor or the president of the student council (although they likely could be), but instead they are individuals known to get the job done and whose opinions are valued. Try to get to know these people. Their advice and guidance can help your transition.

241 Making a funny one

When making any kind of presentation, it is helpful to try to insert some humor into it, particularly if your talk is longer than ten minutes.

Zig Ziglar, a great motivational speaker and author, suggests that an audience's attention span is approximately nine to eleven minutes. Therefore, he tries to get them laughing at least once every ten minutes. A joke or story at the start is usually effective in getting the audience involved in your speech. Regardless of the timing, you don't want to offend your audience. Avoid humor that references sex, religion or race.

242 Be Quiet

Why is it important to say nothing if you don't have anything nice to say?

For three reasons: first of all, nobody likes negative people (not even other negative people). If you habitually say bad things about other individuals or situations, people will avoid you; second, people will come to believe that, because you are prone to say bad things about other people, you are likely to say something bad about them as well;

finally, there is a possibility your comments will be relayed to the person you were talking about, and they will probably not be very happy. Payback may be coming your way.

243 One of the keys to happiness is a bad memory

— Rita Mae Brown (b. 1944)

Don't dwell on the bad things that happen in your life. Granted, some things are difficult to forget. In the case of the passing away of a loved one, remember the person and try to forget the pain. When you flunk a course because you didn't work hard enough, remember the lesson (you didn't work hard enough!) and forget the blow to your self-esteem. If you get dumped by someone you love, remember the good times, but not the way it ended.

Try to forget the bad and remember the good. You will be a more contented person.

244 Introductions

When you are introduced to someone, always extend your hand regardless of their sex and age. If you are seated, always stand up to shake someone's hand.

Men: always stand up if a lady whom you do not know enters the room.

245 Message For Life

The Dalai Lama (b. 1935) has a list of instructions for good living that he calls his "Message For Life." Here are some of them:

Take into account that great love and great achievements involve great risk.

When you lose, don't lose the lesson.

Follow the three Rs:
    Respect for self
    Respect for others
    Responsibility for all your actions.

Remember that not getting what you want is sometimes a wonderful stroke of luck.

Don't let a little dispute injure a great friendship.

When you realize you've made a mistake, take immediate steps to correct it.

Spend some time alone every day.

Open your arms to change, but don't let go of your values.

Remember that silence is sometimes the best answer.

Live a good, honorable life. Then when you get older and think back, you'll be able to enjoy it a second time.

A loving atmosphere in your home is the foundation for your life.

In disagreements with loved ones, deal only with the current situation. Don't bring up the past.

Share your knowledge. It's a way to achieve immortality.

Be gentle with the earth.

Once a year, go someplace you've never been before.

Remember that the best relationship is one in which your love for each other exceeds your need for each other.

Judge your success by what you had to give up in order to get it.

IMAGINATION OVER INTELLIGENCE

246 Never let the fear of striking out get in your way

MONDAY

— *Babe Ruth (1895–1948)*

One of the greatest home-run hitters in baseball history, Babe Ruth, had almost double the number of strikeouts than he did home runs (1,330 strikeouts and 714 home runs). That is, while becoming one of the greatest home-run hitters in baseball, he experienced more failures than successes along the way. Don't let a failure get you down. Step up to the plate and take another swing.

247 I'm so nervous

TUESDAY

Feeling nervous before speaking to a group of people is perfectly normal. In fact, it is a good thing, as it means the speech is important to you and that you care about how the audience responds. Still, you don't want to be so nervous that it takes away from what you are saying, so work to overcome nervousness by keeping the following in mind:

1. **Recognize that you are not alone**. Every public speaker experiences anxiety. Surveys have found that the fear of public speaking is one of the single greatest fears adults have (ranking ahead of heights, death, spiders and confined spaces)[10]. Even top entertainers admit that they get nervous before a performance. Understand that nervousness is a perfectly normal and acceptable emotion, and accept it in yourself.

2. **Realize that people want you to do well**. Audiences want speakers to be interesting, stimulating, informative and entertaining. In general, they want you to succeed, not to fail.

3. **Know your subject matter**. This will build confidence.

4. **Prepare thoroughly**. Nothing reduces anxiety more than the realization that you are well-prepared. Make sure you have mastered your material and know what you are going to say. If you are unprepared, then you deserve to feel nervous.

5. **Concentrate on your message and not on your anxiety**. Your

nervous feelings will dissipate if you focus your attention away from your own anxieties and nervousness; instead, focus outward – toward your message and your audience.

6. **Turn nervousness into positive energy**. The same nervous energy that causes anxiety can be an asset. Harness it and transform it into enthusiasm.

7. **Get experience**. Experience builds confidence.

248 Mistakes are a fact of life. It is the response to error that counts

— *Nikki Giovanni (b. 1943)*

Expect to make mistakes. Just be sure you don't make the same mistake twice.

When a mistake is made, you need to do two things: first, learn from it; and second, respond appropriately. If your mistake has hurt someone, apologize. If your mistake harms your company in some way, own up to it to your superior. If your mistake causes financial hardship, offer to make amends.

Whether the mistake is big or small, you need to respond in an appropriate manner. And that means you don't try to hide it, but rather to correct it.

249 If you tell the truth, you'll never have to be concerned with your memory

If you tend to make up stories, you'll have to have a very good memory because chances are that when you go to tell the story again it will be different. This inconsistency can hurt your credibility. Maintaining credibility with people important to you – your spouse, children, friends, colleagues or employer – is necessary to preserve their respect for you.

250 We cannot direct the wind, but we can adjust the sails

FRIDAY

— *Bertha Calloway*

There are many things over which you will have no control. No matter what they are, though, you can control your response to them. When something unexpected happens, accept it and react to it. Respond to it accordingly and don't let it push you off course.

251 Whenever you enter a room, enter it with confidence

SATURDAY

When you walk in, have a smile on your face, stand tall and, if there are a lot of people, scan the crowd for someone to talk to. Try to become engaged with someone as soon as possible. It helps to look for one of the following: the host; someone you already know; or someone you would like to know. If you don't initially see someone from this list, then look for someone who will appreciate your interest and conversation. These will be people who are standing alone or who look uncomfortable. A sign that someone is uncomfortable is if they are clutching their cup or glass with both hands. Approach these people with a smile, extend your hand and introduce yourself.

252 When you were born, you cried and the world rejoiced. Live your life in such a manner that when you die, the world cries and you rejoice

SUNDAY

— *Indian proverb.*

Live your life so that in your old age you can reflect back on a full, fruitful life. To help achieve this, be at peace with God during your lifetime, such that your words, deeds and beliefs are solid enough that they will help to pave your way into heaven.

As well, we hope to see our family in the next life. Therefore, work throughout your life to make sure your loved ones share this philosophy as well.

253 Progress always involves risk; you can't steal second base and keep your foot on first

— Frederick Wilcox

Sports offer insightful metaphors for teaching life skills. Baseball has more than its fair share of these metaphorical life lessons. In baseball you have failures (strikeouts), you have small successes (base hits), and you have the big triumphs (home runs). There is even risk, such as when you steal second base. For example, in order to successfully steal second base, you have had some success already – you got to first base – and then you had the courage to try to better yourself, even though there was a risk of failure (getting put out), which would nullify your initial success.

Don't be afraid to take risks – calculated ones, not stupid ones.

254 Don't smoke

Aside from the fact that it kills you and the people close to you, it is expensive, and increasingly many employers don't allow smoking in the workplace.

Smoking leaves people with two impressions: that you are prone to unhealthy habits and that you have a lack of will power.

255 Lying

We hope this doesn't happen, but at some point in your working life you may be asked by a superior to lie for them. This will be stressful, for two reasons: first, due to a lack of practice, you will be a poor liar;

and two, you will ultimately have to make a decision about whether you want to work at a place where lying is an accepted part of the culture.

If you are asked to lie, here is a suggested course of action: tell your superior you are uncomfortable lying on their behalf. Explain to them that, if you are able to lie on behalf of them, then you are able to lie to them. And point out that they probably do not want an employee who is prepared and able to tell lies. If your employer does not respond to this position to your satisfaction, start looking for someplace else to work.

256 Talent is God given. Be humble. Fame is man given. Be grateful. Conceit is self given. Be careful.

— *John Wooden (b. 1910)*

257 There is nothing permanent except change

— *Heraclitus (c. 535 BC– 475 BC)*

To paraphrase it: "The only thing constant in life is change." There will be times when you feel secure in your job, in your relationships or on the team. Don't be lulled into a false sense of security. Understand that things will change. Sometimes it is change for the better, but sometimes it is not. Accept that change is a part of life and learn to deal with it. In fact, adopt the attitude that you welcome change, because it means you are alive – both figuratively and literally.

258 Which fork do I use?

Knowing which utensil to use for the various courses of a meal can be confusing.

In general terms, you start with the outermost utensil or utensils for each course and work inward. In a fancy restaurant, you will usually receive only as much silverware as you will need, and it will be arranged in the right order. Typically at a restaurant, as each course is finished the silverware will be removed with the dish, leaving you ready for the next item to arrive. At meals in someone's home, it is proper manners to assume that the host has set the table correctly.

Generally, there will be no more than two forks and two knives at each side of your dinner plate. This means it is unlikely you will have more than two or three courses. On those rare occasions when there are more than three or four courses planned, new silverware will be brought to you after all of the original settings have been used.

Keeping the above in mind, here are some other helpful hints:

Soup: The soup spoon is often (but not always) the only spoon provided at the initial place setting. It is usually round in shape and is placed on the right hand side of your plate on the outside of your knives.

Spaghetti: A spoon is usually provided to help you eat spaghetti. The most accepted way to eat spaghetti is by using your fork to pick up a small pile of the pasta, placing it against the spoon, and twirling it into a compact ball around the end of your fork. Then lift the fork to your mouth. Do not cut the spaghetti with your knife and be careful not to "slurp" when you are eating.

Salad: The salad fork often has a thicker tine on one side of the fork. This strengthens the fork for use in cutting large salad greens without having to resort to using a knife.

Fish: Both a fork and a knife are provided for fish. The fish fork is usually shorter than the meat fork.

Meat: The inside fork and knife are to be used for any meat served during the meal.

Dessert: The dessert fork or spoon is often brought in with the dessert. If not, they are usually placed horizontally at the top of the plate and parallel to each other, with the bowl of the spoon pointing to the left and the tines of the fork pointing right. If coffee and tea are served, a teaspoon will likely be served with the saucer.

If you are ever in doubt about what utensils to use, watch what your host does; failing that, do what your immediate table neighbors are doing.

Here is an example of a table setting to help you out:

1. The dinner plate.
2. The napkin.
3. The dinner fork.
4. The salad fork.
5. The salad plate.
6. The dinner knife (with the blade edge facing the plate).
7. The dinner spoon.
8. The soup spoon.
9. The dessert spoon (the bowl facing opposite the tines of the dessert fork).
10. The dessert fork (with the tines to the right).
11. The bread plate (placed at the 11 o'clock position with respect to the dinner plate).
12. A small butter knife (usually placed diagonally across the bread plate).
13. A water goblet (placed at the one o'clock position with respect to the dinner plate).
14. The red wine glass (placed just in front and to the right of the water glass).
15. The white wine glass (placed just in front and to the right of the red wine glass).

259 Heaven's entrance exam

When your time here on earth is over and you are standing at the

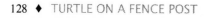

gates of heaven, be prepared to provide an accounting of your life. Be prepared to answer some questions. Fortunately, St. Peter has done us a favor by sending out a cheat sheet.

- God won't ask what kind of car you drove, He'll ask how many people you drove who didn't have transportation.
- God won't ask the square footage of your house, He'll ask how many people you welcomed into your home.
- God won't ask about the clothes you had in your closet, He'll ask how many you helped to clothe.
- God won't ask what your highest salary was, He'll ask if you compromised your character to obtain it.
- God won't ask what your job title was, He'll ask if you performed your job to the best of your ability.
- God won't ask how many friends you had, He'll ask how many people to whom you were a friend.
- God won't ask in what neighborhood you lived, He'll ask how you treated your neighbors.
- God won't ask about the color of your skin, He'll ask about the content of your character.

— Author Unknown

260 If you put off everything until you are sure of it, you will get nothing done

MONDAY

— Norman Vincent Peale (1898–1993)

When making a decision, it is tempting to wait until you have more information. However, the reality is that you will never get all the information you think you need. Decision-making is a balancing act between considering only the information you have and waiting until you have more. You must develop the ability to take whatever information you have at the moment, analyze it and make a decision. This is not to suggest you should be flippant about making big decisions; after all, decisions on choosing a university, changing employers or buying a house are huge, and research needs to be done before you make a final selection. In reality, though, most decisions will have to be made without having "all" the information.

261 A dream is just a dream. A goal is a dream with a plan and a deadline

— *Harvey Mackay (b. 1932)*

The world is full of dreamers. Graduates enter the working world dreaming of becoming CEOs, or starting a business and becoming millionaires, or being a school principal, or building a hospital in Africa. What too many dreamers don't have, however, is a well thought-out plan to help them achieve their dreams. Dreams don't just simply come true because you want them to; they take planning.

To achieve your dreams, you have to work hard and you have to work smart. Having a plan is smart. A well thought-out, written-down plan serves as a road map. Make sure you prepare one.

262 Never be late for a business meeting or appointment

Always arrive early for these events... five minutes ahead of time is sufficient. If an unforeseen event occurs that will cause you to be late, you must phone ahead to let others know you will not be on time for the meeting.

Being late without calling ahead with a valid reason leaves the impression that you think the other person's time is not as important as yours.

263 Don't let success OR failure go to your head

You will experience both in your life. When you have a success, internalize it. In your mind, create a "Bank of Success" in which you deposit your wins. By internalizing your success rather than vocalizing it, your success will not morph into arrogance. Rather, internalizing it will help you to grow in confidence. More importantly, the next time you do experience failure, you can afford to make a withdrawal from your "Bank of Success" to counteract it. As long as you've made enough deposits, any withdrawal will be inconsequential to your bank account balance.

264 The Echo Of Life

When Uncle Doug was a very young boy, he and Grandpa Frank were walking in the forest near a big cliff. Uncle tripped over a rock and scraped his knee. "Ouch!" he screamed.

He heard a voice yell back from across the valley, "Ouch!"

Filled with curiosity, he yelled, "Who are you?" The answer he received back was, "Who are you?"

Thinking someone was teasing him, he became angry and screamed, "Shut up, you jerk!" to which the voice answered, "Shut up, you jerk!"

Uncle Doug looked at Grandpa Frank and said, "Dad, what is going on?"

"Son," he replied, "pay attention!"

Then he yelled, "I admire you!"

The voice answered, "I admire you!"

Grandpa shouted, "You are wonderful!" and the voice answered, "You are wonderful!"

Uncle Doug was surprised, but still didn't understand what was happening.

Then Grandpa explained, "Some people call this an echo. But it is really life. Understand that life gives you back what you give out – it is a mirror of your actions."

Grandpa went on to say, "If you want more kindness, give more kindness. If you want understanding and respect, give understanding and respect. If you want people to be patient and respectful toward you, give patience and respect. This applies to every aspect of your life."

— *Author Unknown*

265 Becoming a good conversationalist

SATURDAY

If you want to be a good conversationalist, it helps to be wr^2; "**wr** squared" means **w**ell **r**ead and **w**ell **r**ounded.

A well-informed person can make good conversation in any situation. To help you become well informed, you should try to read at least two newspapers each day (a local one and a national one). This will help to build your knowledge base and give you insight into current events.

It is also a good idea to read up on a number of different subjects. Take an interest in reading about the arts, theatre, movies, politics, books and sports. If you have some general knowledge about these topics, you will be able to have lively discussions and pose intelligent questions in virtually any situation.

A cautionary note, however: no one likes a know-it-all. Use your knowledge to help you be a part of the conversation, but not to dominate one.

266 God doesn't make junk

SUNDAY

— *Ethel Waters (1896–1977)*

There will be times in your life when you don't feel very good about yourself. Times when your body image doesn't meet your expectations (whose does!); or when you have a string of bad luck at work or at school; or when you get dumped by someone. When you face those times and are feeling down, remember who made you.

Another lesson to take away from this quote is that every person is a creation of God. Every person has value as a human being, therefore every person has something you can learn from. There is something positive in everyone even though their actions might suggest otherwise.

If you find yourself in a position in which you must work with someone you don't like, challenge yourself to find the good in that person. This approach will help you see their positive attributes, thus making it easier to do your job.

267 It is actually a good thing to have some setbacks in your life

MONDAY

Setbacks and failures can be grouped into two types: good and bad. Try to avoid the bad ones and embrace the good ones.

The bad ones are things like marital breakdowns, alcohol and drug addiction, and promiscuity. The good ones are mistakes that occurred because you challenged yourself: you got cut from the varsity team; you didn't get the job promotion you were after; you didn't get into the grad school you had chosen.

Develop a mindset that good failures aren't setbacks at all, but life lessons. As well, understand that if you are not experiencing good failures, it means you are not challenging yourself. Don't feel ashamed of those setbacks; view them as a "badge of honor."

268 How to be a good conversationalist

TUESDAY

When you finish a conversation with someone you have just met, whether at a business function or at a social gathering, ask yourself this: "Did I learn more about the other person than they learned about me?" The answer will tell you if you are a good conversationalist.

People like to talk about themselves. If you learned more about the other person than they learned about you, it meant they did most of the talking. If this is the case, they will think you're a good conversation-alist. They will feel good about the conversation and will view you in a favorable light.

269 The best remedy for anger is delay

— Brigham Young (1801–1877)

Always remember the 24-hour rule when you get angry. If you respond immediately, you may regret your response.

If you receive an email or a voice mail that makes you angry, do not respond for 24 hours. Sleep on it. That extra time will help you to cool down a bit, and give you the chance to look at the situation from other perspectives. This will help you to prepare a measured, thoughtful response.

270 Real generosity is doing something nice for someone who will never find it out

— Frank A. Clark

You have a duty to help better the lives of others. Expect nothing in return for your efforts. Be willing to help even if your efforts do not get recognized. While other people may not see your efforts, two important people will know of them: you and God.

271 Memorizing what you read

If you need to memorize a lot of text, such as when you are studying for an exam, remember the **PQ4R** method. Developed by Robert Slavin[11], **PQ4R** stands for **p**review, **q**uestion, and then the **4 R**s: **r**ead, **r**eflect, **r**ecite and **r**eview.

The **PQ4R** method is based on the premise that your brain becomes very focused when it is presented with a question.

The first step is to **p**review the text by reviewing the table of contents and then looking at any headings. Then you form **q**uestions about the text by converting the headlines to questions. If there are no headlines, convert the first sentences of the major paragraphs.

You next go through the 4 **R**s: **R**ead the text carefully, trying to answer the questions you created. **R**eflect on what you have read by attempting to apply any principles you have just read. Then **r**ecite the material you just covered – either verbally or by summarizing it in written form. Finally, **r**eview the text again, trying to recall what you have read and summarizing the main points.

272 Ha Ha Ha Ha!

It is important to practise telling jokes or stories, particularly the punch lines. It can be embarrassing to flub a punch line or tell a boring story. If you can't tell a joke well, then spare everyone and don't tell it.

Keep in mind that jokes must be appropriate for the circumstances. Humor must be **TACT**:

Tasteful: Don't slur anyone or any group and don't embarrass anyone by telling off-color jokes or stories;

Appropriate: The joke or story should have relevance to your conversation;

Concise: The joke or story should not be too long; and

Timely: The story or joke should have relevance to recent events.

273 Using your imagination

Remember when you were young and could play for hours using only your imagination? Adults still have an imagination, but unfortunately we tend to use it the wrong way.

Our adult imaginations often cause us to worry about things that never happen. When anticipating something, we tend to picture the worst-case scenario, when in reality things rarely end up being as bad as imagined. Sometimes these things don't even happen at all.

It is healthy to be concerned about upcoming events because it shows concern. But don't let this concern turn into worry. Worry is a negative emotion that robs you of focus, confidence and sleep. The Bible asks the question: "And which of you by worrying can add a single hour to his life's span?" (Luke 12:25). The answer is: no one. Therefore, don't worry yourself into a frenzy. More times than not, you will look back and wonder why you got so worked up in the first place.

Mark Twain (1835–1910) said: "I am an old man and have known a great many troubles, but most of them never happened."

274 The lens of fear magnifies the size of the uncertainty

MONDAY

— *Dr. Charles Swindoll (b. 1934)*

No question, things are more difficult when you are afraid. The first time you stood at the top of the ski hill looking down, you had visions of a painful crash, but after a few tentative trips down the hill you became more comfortable and were not nearly as afraid. Your doubts subsided.

The same can be said for other things – public speaking, first dates, heading off to university. The more afraid you are, the greater your doubts. Don't let fear or doubt hinder you. The exception to this rule is when there is a possibility of physical danger. Then it is good to be cautious.

Make a habit of seeing life through the right kind of eyeglasses: those that help you see the opportunity, not the ones that magnify the fear.

275 Touching people

If you are a "toucher," be careful in a corporate setting. When it comes to physically touching people in a corporate environment, less is more. Most of the time, light touching conveys warmth and openness to people. But you must be careful, as many people are uncomfortable being touched by someone else. In those cases, avoid any extra touching after the initial handshake. You'll have to gauge people's receptiveness to touching. If they seem uncomfortable, stop immediately. With others, you can be a bit "touchy," subject to a couple of conditions.

When you are unmarried, it's okay to lightly touch a member of the opposite sex after the initial handshake. As noted, in a business setting the touch should not linger. In a social setting, the touch can linger, especially if you want to send a message. In the business environment, as a single man it is acceptable to touch other men on the shoulders and to touch women on the forearm. As a single woman, it is usually acceptable to touch both men and women on the arm. But, again, remember to keep the touching "light."

If you are married, it is a good idea to avoid touching the opposite sex altogether, except for the initial handshake. In today's business (and litigious) environment, avoid sending out signals that could be misconstrued.

276 Take a load off

In one of his classes, Grandpa Frank raised a glass of water and asked, "How heavy is this glass of water?"

The answers called out ranged from 20g to 500g. Grandpa Frank replied, "The weight doesn't matter. It depends on how long you try to hold it."

"If I hold it for a minute, that's not a problem. If I hold it for an hour,

...AND OTHERS WILL RESPECT YOU

I'll have an ache in my right arm. If I hold it for a day, you'll have to call an ambulance for me. In each case, it's the same weight, but the longer I hold it, the heavier it becomes."

He went on, "And that's the way it is with handling stress. If we carry our burdens around all the time, sooner or later the burden becomes increasingly heavier and we won't be able to carry on.

"Just like with this glass of water, put it down and rest for a while. When you're refreshed, you can carry on.

"Whatever burdens you're carrying now, find some way to let them down for a moment.

"Learn to relax and deal with them later, after you've rested."

— *Author Unknown*

277 One moment of patience may ward off great disaster; one moment of impatience may ruin a whole life

— *Chinese proverb*

While this message may apply to a number of things, consider it as it applies to pre-marital sex. The only 100% guaranteed method to avoid getting pregnant and to avoid catching sexually transmitted infections (STIs) is abstinence.

An unwanted pregnancy for an unmarried couple can have a significant effect on many lives. STIs have their own severe implications: they can cause embarrassment, pain, sterility and even death.

Are there other methods of birth and disease control? Yes, there are. Condoms seem to be the most popular. However, you should know that they are not without risk.

Many STIs, including HIV, the virus that causes AIDS, are tiny organisms that are much smaller than sperm. A 1992 paper in *Applied and Environmental Microbiology* found that HIV is three times smaller than the herpes virus, 60 times smaller than syphilis and anywhere from 50 to 450 times smaller than sperm[12]. Consequently, if a condom is not used properly – or even worse if it has a hole – STIs have a greater chance of escaping from the condom.

Over the years, there have been a number of research studies that have looked at the failure rates of condoms. A 1993 University of Texas study analyzed the results of 11 different studies that had tracked the effectiveness of condoms to prevent transmission of the AIDS virus. The average condom failure rate in the 11 studies was 31%[13]. Similarly, there was a study by the U.S. Food and Drug Administration that tested condoms in a laboratory for leakage of HIV-sized particles. Almost 33% of the condoms leaked.[14]

One of the major reasons condoms can fail in preventing the transfer of AIDS is that latex condoms have tiny holes called "voids." Sperm is generally larger than these voids, but the AIDS virus can be up to ten times smaller than these tiny holes, and thus it is possible for the virus to pass through[15]. Think about it. Would you get on an airplane if you knew it had a 30% chance of breaking down while you were flying?

The failure rate for condoms in preventing pregnancy is also quite high. Various studies have put the failure rate at 10%–15%.[16] In many people's eyes, this is an unacceptably high failure rate given the potential consequences.

Now, using a condom is better than nothing. But understand that for a single person there is really no "safe sex." What you should do is "save sex" – for marriage.

The human sex drive is very powerful. Do not put yourself in a position where one moment of weakness can lead to life-altering consequences.

278 We are shaped and fashioned by what we love

— J.W. von Goethe (1749–1832)

If you love money, money will control you. If you love fame, you will yearn for it. If you strive for power, power will define you.

Make sure that what you love is meaningful. Things like family, health and your God are important. In the big picture, fame, big houses or fancy cars are not.

279 Pass the bread please

SATURDAY

When you are passed the breadbasket at the dinner table, take only one slice of bread or one bun at a time. If the bread is in the form of a loaf, it is acceptable to rip the bread from the loaf with your hands; but be neat about it. With a bun, don't cut it open but rather gently tear it open with your hands.

When buttering your bread or bun, follow these guidelines:

1. If there is a butter knife, use it to take a section of the butter and put it on your bread plate. Don't put the butter directly onto your bread using the butter knife. It's done this way so you'll have your own butter on your plate and won't have to continually use the communal butter dish;

2. Next, tear off a small piece of your bread (one or two bites' worth); and

3. Finally, butter the bite-sized piece using your own knife and the butter from your plate.

280 For everyone who exalts themselves will be humbled, and he who humbles himself will be exalted

SUNDAY

— Luke 14:11

Despite the fact that the media likes to showcase the arrogance of today's professional athletes and corporate leaders, it is better to keep a low profile and to stay low-key. Don't call attention to yourself, for two reasons: first, it is unbecoming (most people don't like arrogance); and second, you will set yourself up for people to take shots at you.

Be modest. Over time, modesty earns respect.

281 Failure is only the opportunity to begin again more intelligently

— Henry Ford (1863–1947)

Failure means you were trying to do something that was difficult. It meant you were trying to stretch yourself. And that is commendable.

However, make sure that when you do have a setback, you learn something from it. Don't fail again because you didn't learn something the first time.

282 A leader wants to know

One of the reasons why Genghis Khan – the conqueror of much of Asia and Eastern Europe in the 1200s – had success was that he was innovative. He would try something new and unexpected, and this would throw off his enemies.

Like any good leader, he knew there would be some setbacks. He was prepared to make mistakes. His strength was that he encouraged discussion about the failures and, most importantly, he would listen. He removed impediments to the truth reaching him. Effective leaders know they don't know it all. Part of their success comes from creating an environment that encourages openness. This means discussing what the group is doing right – and what the group is doing wrong. A true leader wants to be made aware of the "warts," for if you can't see 'em, you can't fix 'em.

Make sure, when leading a group, team, organization or company, that your people understand that occasional setbacks are an acceptable cost of moving forward. Moreover, strive to create a culture that encourages people to bring to your attention any setbacks. Discuss them and learn from them.

...IT IS CHEAP MEDICINE

283 The Crow and the Rabbit

There is a story about a crow sitting on top of a tree doing nothing. A small rabbit sees the crow and asks him, "Can I also sit like you and do nothing all day long?" The crow answers, "Sure, why not." So the rabbit sits on the ground below the crow and rests. All of a sudden, a fox appears, attacks the rabbit and eats it. The moral of the story is said to be this: to be sitting and doing nothing, you must be sitting very, very, high up.

While this story may be good for a few laughs (okay, not very many), you need to understand that the underlying message is blatantly wrong. Senior people should never be seen to be doing nothing. Whomever you are – the CEO, the captain of the team, the choir conductor – you must always be seen to be working hard. The tone is set from the top. If you sit around, others will follow your lead and do the same thing. If you are active, they will be active. Make sure you set the proper example.

284 It's too good to be true

If something seems too good to be true, then it probably is. There is always free cheese in a mousetrap.

We live in a very competitive world. Lots of competition usually results in a level playing field. Whether it pertains to investment returns, holiday vacation packages, or a used car, if the price seems too good, you'd better take a harder look because there is probably more to the story.

There is a concept that applies to the stock market called "efficient markets." It is the belief that all relevant information about a company is available and has been disclosed to the public. The theory is that everyone is equally informed about the firm's prospects, and therefore the stock price should be valued fairly. Granted, some people do have access to undisclosed (inside) information that can give them an advantage and an ability to profit unduly. However, using this information to profit is illegal. Thus, the assumption is made that the share price is fair. This concept – the efficient markets theory – applies to most things in our everyday life as well. Because of the huge effect the internet has had on getting information out to the public, and given the competitive nature of our society in general, there are very few instances in which any of us gets something of value for less than what it is actually worth. Hence the reason to be wary if something appears too good to be true. There may be an unpleasant surprise attached to it.

285 Death and taxes

You may have heard the phrase "The only sure things in life are death and taxes." Often this is said in a negative context. Thinking of death and taxes negatively is actually the wrong attitude.

First of all, you will die. There is absolutely nothing you can do to change that – so why feel stress about it. If you live a fulfilled, spiritual life, you have nothing to fear. Your next stop will be even better than this one.

Second, there is nothing wrong with paying taxes. It means you are making money. The more tax you pay, the better the standard of living you have (if you don't, change your accountant). Look forward to the day when you will pay $1 million in taxes – just think what your total income will be!

286 R.S.V.P.

When you receive any kind of invitation, practice good manners from the time you receive the invitation until after you have left the function.

Here are the basics:

1. RSVP is an abbreviation for "respond, please" in French. Respond if you are asked to, regardless if your answer is yes or no;

2. Treat everyone at the function nicely whether their title impresses you or not;

3. Always thank the host before leaving; and

4. Send a handwritten "thank you" note after the event is over.

287 Anyway

— by Mother Teresa (1910–1997)

People are unreasonable, illogical and self-centered.
Love them anyway.

If you do good, people will accuse you of selfish ulterior motives.
Do good anyway.

If you are successful, you win false friends and true enemies.
Succeed anyway.

The good you do today will be forgotten tomorrow.
Do good anyway.

Honesty and frankness make you vulnerable.
Be honest and frank anyway.

What you spend years building may be destroyed overnight.
Build anyway.

People really need help but may attack you if you help them.
Help people anyway.

Give the world the best you have and you'll get kicked in the teeth.
Give the world the best you've got anyway.

You see, in the final analysis, it is between you and God.
It was never between you and them.

288 It isn't the mountains ahead that wear you out, it's the grain of sand in your shoe

MONDAY

— *Chinese proverb*

Make sure you deal with problems as soon as they occur. Many big problems started out tiny. Attack problems early, while they are still small enough to deal with. Don't let things fester until they grow into something that can cause real damage.

289 Never drink in front of your boss

TUESDAY

Never drink too much alcohol at a business event. In fact, it is best not to drink any.

Getting drunk or even "tipsy" at a work function shows poor judgment and a lack of control. This type of behavior will be perceived negatively by your colleagues and (more importantly) the senior people in the organization. Too much alcohol can lead you to do and say things that are embarrassing or downright stupid. Many careers have been derailed by having too much Christmas "spirit" at the company party.

290 Giving advice

WEDNESDAY

The secret to giving advice is knowing when to stop. Even better, it is best not to start, especially with your work colleagues.

Unless people ask for your advice explicitly, don't offer any. Nobody likes unsolicited advice.

The only people who actually listen to unsolicited advice are your children. And that stops when they become teenagers. ☺

...YOU KNOW MORE THAN YOU THINK YOU DO

291 Always be a little kinder than necessary

— Jim Barrie (1860–1937)

It is very good to be kind to people. It is great to be kinder than necessary. Giving people more effort than what they expect results in them thinking highly of you. Giving people more kindness than they expect will surprise them. Don't be afraid to surprise people.

292 Gossip hurts

One time, when she was in grade six, Auntie Cheri was caught by Grandpa Frank gossiping and spreading rumors about one of her classmates. When he heard her, he asked her to come to his office. Auntie Cheri was terrified because she knew that Grandpa Frank did not tolerate gossip; he thought it was hurtful and unnecessary. She knew she was going to be taught a lesson and that it probably wouldn't be a pleasant one. However, to her surprise, instead of getting punished when she went into his office, Grandpa Frank made Auntie play darts.

He put a picture of the classmate in the center of the dart board and had her throw darts at it. After five minutes or so, once the picture was completely pockmarked with holes and virtually destroyed, he took down the picture and showed it to her. Auntie felt bad seeing how the darts had messed up her friend's face. Auntie anticipated that the lesson Grandpa Frank was going to teach her was that gossip had the same effect on people as the darts did on the picture. It hurt people and made them look bad.

She was only partly right. He turned the picture of her friend over and on the back was another one – a picture of Grandpa Frank – which was, of course, now also full of holes. He told Auntie to remember that every time she gossiped about someone, she hurt Grandpa Frank as well, because he believed that kind of behavior was wrong.

— Author Unknown

293 Eating with your fingers

SATURDAY

When is it appropriate to use your fingers at a sit-down meal? In general, if it has a bone you can use your fingers; otherwise use your knife and fork.

The exceptions to this rule of thumb are the following:

Bread should be broken rather than cut with a knife. Tear off a piece that is about two bites' worth and eat that before tearing off another (see Day 279 for more details).

Cookies should be picked up and eaten.

Corn on the cob may be picked up. Butter one or two rows at a time and eat across the cob cleanly.

Potato chips, French fries and **hamburgers** are intended to be eaten with your hands, although if you come across a particularly messy hamburger you should use a fork and knife. Steak fries (the big, thick, less crispy fries) should be eaten with a fork.

Hors d'oeuvres. Almost everything that is served at a cocktail party or during the pre-meal cocktail hour is meant to be eaten with your fingers. Some of these types of foods are also served during the meal. If they are, it is okay to use your fingers to eat them. This includes olives, pickles, nuts and deviled eggs.

Lobster and **crab claws** are to be picked up with your hands (see Day 363 for details on eating lobsters).

Sandwiches are intended to be picked up to be eaten. The exception is if they are the large open-faced sandwiches that are too big to fit into your mouth. In this case, use a fork and knife.

Small fruits and **berries** with their stems still on (strawberries with the hulls on, cherries with stems, or grapes in bunches) are to be eaten with your fingers. Otherwise you should use a spoon. Sometimes when there are grapes served there may be a small set of scissors as well.

Use these scissors to cut off a small cluster of grapes from the bunch. If there are no scissors, tear off a branch from the whole rather than plucking off single grapes.

294 If anyone competes as an athlete, he does not win the prize unless he competes according to the rules

SUNDAY

— 2 Timothy 2:5

This applies to sports and business. Make sure you play by the rules or else you will never be a winner, no matter how many trophies you win or how much money you make.

295 When we are no longer able to change a situation, we are challenged to change ourselves

MONDAY

— Viktor Frankl (1905–1997), in Man's Search for Meaning

There will be times when you must be prepared to make changes in order to preserve something that is important to you. Your marriage and your health are just two things that are worthy of your making changes in order to ensure success. If addictions such as alcohol, drugs, gambling or too much golf cause difficulties in your marriage, take whatever action is necessary to make it right. If your quick temper causes you to be overlooked for job promotions, control it. If your roommate's all-night partying causes you to do poorly in school, make changes to the living arrangements.

Regardless of what needs to be done, look to yourself to make changes when necessary; don't rely on others to make them for you.

296 Two is better than one

God gave us two ears and two eyes but only one mouth. Why? Because you learn more by listening with your two ears or by observing with your two eyes than by talking with your one mouth.

In the workplace, don't be overly talkative. Instead, listen and observe.

297 People like positive people

One way to convey your "positivity" from the outset (from the start of the day, the start of the meeting, the start of the conversation) is to have a positive response to the question "how are you?" Have one ready to go that highlights your positive outlook. Even better is if it helps people remember you. Some options include the following:

"Awesome."

"Dandy."

"If I was any better I'd be twins."

"Today I'm great, but I'm looking forward to tomorrow." Why? "Because I get better every day."

These responses will often get a smile and a positive comment back. And that's a good way to start any interaction.

298 Accept the fact that everyone makes mistakes

That's why there are erasers on pencils and "delete" keys on computers. This knowledge should apply to both yourself and your attitude toward your friends, loved ones, colleagues and teammates; no one is mistake-free. And while it may be frustrating to be affected by a mistake, understand that they are a part of life. Don't be too harsh.

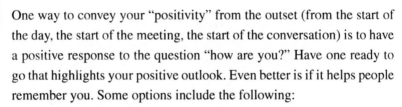

299 The Bird in the Manure

A little bird was flying south for the winter. It was very cold, and partway through his journey it froze and fell to the ground in a large farmer's field. While it was lying there almost dead, a cow came by and dropped a "cow pie" on it. As the frozen bird lay there in the pile of manure, it began to realize how much warmer it was. In fact, the manure actually started to thaw him out! The bird was so happy he began to sing with joy. A passing cat heard the singing and came over to investigate. Following the singing, the cat discovered the bird in the manure, dug him out, and… ate him.

There are a couple of lessons to be taken away from this story:

1. Not everyone who you think "craps" on you is your enemy. You may think they are being unkind, but examine their motives before reacting as they may be trying to help;

2. Not everyone who gets you out of trouble is your friend. Make sure that when you get into trouble, the people who offer to help have your best interests at heart; and

3. Finally, when you are in deep doo-doo, keep your mouth shut. Fix the problem and do not bring attention to it.

— *Author Unknown*

300 Networking

When you are at a social function that has potential networking benefits, try to position yourself strategically between the room entrance and either the finger-food table or the bar. This way, everybody has to walk by you to get to the food or drink, giving you the opportunity to make eye contact or engage in conversation.

301 A fool always loses his temper, but a wise man holds it back

— Proverbs 29:11

Nobody likes to see someone losing their temper. Losing your temper shows an inability to retain control. Most people, including employers, will view it as a sign of weakness.

302 When we long for life without difficulties, remind us that oaks grow strong in contrary winds and diamonds are made under pressure

— Peter Marshall (1902–1949)

Sometimes we wish for life to be easier. But the "easy" life is dull. Consider the many examples of people who retire, only to "unretire" soon after because they are bored and need challenges. Or consider sports teams – the ones that achieve greatness are those that consistently play against the toughest competition.

We need to face difficulties in our lives in order to grow and improve. If you are not challenging yourself continually, you will stagnate. Remember, your competition is striving to improve – so must you. Ergo, embrace difficulties.

303 Be wary of certain words

There are words or phrases that people will often use to try to make things appear minor or not very important, when in reality the opposite may be true. By using these phrases, they are trying, consciously or unconsciously, to deflect your attention away from something. If you hear someone use phrases such as "by the way" or "incidentally" at the start of a sentence, consider the possibility that they may be trying to downplay something that is actually important.

304 Comparison destroys contentment

WEDNESDAY

Avoid comparing yourself to others. Understand that your life is unique and that no two people share the identical set of skills, up-bringing, ambitions or willingness to make sacrifices. It is not fair, therefore, to compare your life to theirs.

Someone may work eighty hours per week versus your fifty. If this is the case, they will get more work done and will climb the corporate ladder faster.

Someone may study four hours per day to your two. If this is the case, they will get better marks.

Someone may practise the piano for two hours per day to your one. They will be a better piano player than you.

Because there are so many variables involved in success – work ethic, talent, coaching, attitude, luck – it is impossible for two people to be the same. Accordingly, do not compare yourself with others. It is a game you cannot win, because no one is playing on the exact same field.

If you believe you have done your best, accept that and be content. Avoid the "if onlys": if only I had his job, if only I had her looks, if only I had more money. Don't compare your situation to that of others. You've likely heard of the expression "the grass is always greener on the other side of the fence." Don't believe it. It may appear that way only because the other side has bulls**t spread all over it.

305 Neither a borrower nor a lender be; for a loan oft loses both itself and friend

THURSDAY

— William Shakespeare (1564–1616)

Try to avoid lending money *to* friends and never borrow money *from* friends. Simple as that. Money changes the dynamics of a friendship. When there is money involved, an underlying feeling of "obligation" will develop in the friendship, and this will cause you to question motives: is he helping me build my fence as a friend or because he owes me money? Is she helping me move apartments because she wants to, or because she feels she has to? Once this feeling of obligation enters a friendship, strain and suffering result. Proverbs 22:7 says: "And the borrower becomes the lender's slave." It is difficult for a friendship to survive this.

If you feel compelled to lend money to friends, do it with the expectation that you will not get it back. This way, you won't lose a friend and you won't lose your money (because it was a gift).

The one exception to this rule is if you are making a bona fide investment in a business venture. Then you can do it, but only if the proper paperwork is put in place by professional advisors.

306 Minds are like parachutes. They work best when open

FRIDAY

— *Sir Thomas Dewar (1864–1930)*

There are over six billion people in the world. This means there are six billion opinions, perspectives and viewpoints. It makes practical sense to consider that there may be other ways of doing things, not just your own.

Be willing to consider other possibilities. Be open and don't be too set in your ways.

307 Table manners

SATURDAY

Once you've begun using your knife, fork or spoon, they shouldn't touch the table again.

Once used, don't lean the knife or fork against the plate – it's not acceptable to have even the clean handle of a knife or fork rest on the tablecloth while the other end lies on the plate. Similarly, you should

...WONDERFUL FAIRYTALE OF ALL

not put your knife or fork back in its original place once used. The reason is that they could dirty the tablecloth and result in a cleaning bill for the host.

Another table manner to remember is that, at the end of a course, any used utensil should be left on a flat dish. For example, don't leave a spoon or fork in the soup bowl, in a shrimp cocktail dish, in a coffee cup, or in a desert bowl. Bowls and cups are usually presented with a plate underneath; put the used utensil on this plate when you are done.

308 A jug fills drop by drop

— Buddha (c. 563 BC–c. 483 BC)

Understand that many things take time to come to fruition. Have patience and work diligently, and your goal will be achieved – even if it takes longer than you wanted.

309 To remain number one, train like you are number two

— Maurice Greene (b. 1974)

Once you reach the pinnacle – graduating on the Dean's List, being cast in a play, having a bestseller on the book charts – don't stop trying to get better.

You must continue to work just as hard to stay on top as you did to get there. Otherwise your stay up there won't be very long.

310 Here are two tips for using visual aids effectively in a presentation

1. **Make sure they are visible.**

    The letters should be large and easily readable. Use plenty

of spacing between words. Display the visuals high enough so that everyone in the audience or around the boardroom table can see them, and avoid blocking them out by standing in front of them or the projector. Before your presentation, make a point of testing their visibility by viewing them from various spots in the room.

2. **Keep them simple.**

Make any graphs or diagrams simple and accurate, being sure to give a title to each and labeling the important components of the graph. If you have writing on your visuals, follow the "7–7 rule": ensure there are no more than seven lines per slide and no more than seven words per line.

311 You don't have to explain something you never said

WEDNESDAY

— *Calvin Coolidge (1872–1933)*

Be discreet in what you say and to whom you say it. Don't gossip and don't say more than you need to. In the business world, the less said the better.

312 You can't go looking for happiness. You won't find it

THURSDAY O₂

Many people think that more money, more power or more sex will make them happier. They are wrong. Happiness results from making honest choices and taking honest and prudent actions. If you choose the right lifestyle or job, you will be happy. If you choose the wrong lifestyle (drugs, alcohol, promiscuity, crime), happiness will always elude you.

313 There are two sides to every story

That is why our judicial system requires both sides to be heard. Every judge will tell you that it is very easy to make a decision in a case – that is, until they hear the other side of the story.

Do not rush to judgment until you hear and understand both sides of the story.

314 The Dress Code

If you are invited to a social function and unsure of the dress code, always err on the side of being overdressed. This shows respect for your host.

"Black tie" means formal wear: tuxedos and gowns; "black tie optional" means either formal or semi-formal, meaning at minimum a dark suit/tie or evening dress; "business attire" means suit and tie for men and a conservative dress or business suit for women; "business casual" means a sport coat and slacks for men, and slacks, a conservative top and/or a blazer for women; "casual" means whatever you are comfortable in. Avoid wearing jeans unless you wear a sport coat or blazer and the jeans are in good shape.

315 A man's true wealth is the good he does in this world

— *Muhammad (570–632)*

In the grand scheme of things, it doesn't matter how many cars you have, how big your house is or how large your investment portfolio is. You are rich no matter how little you have if you have a legacy of good works and charity.

J.H. Jowett said: "The real measure of our wealth is how much we'd be worth if we lost all our money."

Every once in a while, ask yourself: how much am I worth?

316 Never be intimidated to try something new just because you don't know much about it

Remember that amateurs built the Ark. Professionals built the Titanic.

Be willing to try new things.

317 Don't specialize too soon

In the early days of your career, you should focus on two things: developing your technical skills and expanding your resume. Try to gain as much experience as possible across all functions of the company or organization. This includes finance, marketing, operations, sales and human resources. When you are just starting out, be prepared to forgo a higher-paying specialist job for one in which you get broad exposure to different areas of the organization. If possible, try to enter a training program that covers all areas. Your career will be a long one – perhaps 40 to 50 years – so don't be too eager to specialize too soon.

318 Associate yourself with men of good quality if you esteem your own reputation, for it is better to be alone than in bad company

— *George Washington (1732–1799)*

If you care about your reputation (and you should), make sure you do some research on your prospective employer. You should be just as careful about choosing your employer as your employer is about choosing you. If you work for an organization with a bad reputation, you may end up with a bad reputation as well. Always keep in mind that you are judged by the company you keep; make sure the verdict works in your favor.

...TO FOLLOW THROUGH

319 Good humor makes all things tolerable

THURSDAY

— *Henry Ward Beecher (1813–1887)*

Cultivate your sense of humor.

This not only means having a good repertoire of jokes, but also the ability to laugh at yourself and to laugh when faced with difficult situations. Laughing is a positive emotion. When you do something stupid, or when you have to do something not very pleasant, try to find the humor in it. The enjoyment you get from laughing – brief as it may be – will help compensate for the embarrassment or unpleasantness of the task.

320 The trouble with being in the rat race is that even if you win, you're still a rat

FRIDAY

— *Lily Tomlin (b. 1939)*

It seems a cliché, but life is like a race. It has a starting line, a finish line and a whole bunch of running in between. Because of this, be sure to choose the right race. There is the one in which everybody is running after nicer homes, fancier cars or bigger flat-screen TVs. Unfortunately, this is a race you can never win because someone will always have something bigger or fancier.

Instead of running in this (rat) race, choose to run in the human race. In the human race, you still enjoy the nicer things in life, but the focus is on things such as making time for your family, practicing your faith and raising well-adjusted children. The nice thing about this race is that the winner is not decided by anyone but you. You set the pace and you determine the finish line. And because you do, this is a race you can win easily.

321 Ordering a bottle of wine

SATURDAY

When you order a bottle of wine at a restaurant, the waiter will bring you the bottle, show you the label side (to ensure it is the bottle you ordered), and then pour a small amount into your glass for you to test.

To test the wine, pick up the glass by the stem and make a circular motion so that the wine moves around in the bowl of the glass. Next, smell the wine by putting your nose directly into the bowl of glass and inhaling. Depending on the type of wine, you will generally detect one or more of the following aromas:[17]

Wine	Aroma
	FRUIT
Chardonnay, some Chenin blanc	Apple
Sémillon	Apricot
young red wines, some Beaujolais	Banana
Pinot noir	Black cherry
common in red wine	Black fruit
Cabernet Sauvignon, some Syrah	Black currant
young red wine	Berries
some Cabernet Franc	Blueberry
red Rhone	Cranberry
unripe Chardonnay	Citrus
Sémillon, some oak Chardonnay	Figs
Sauvignon blanc, Gewurztanimer	Grapefruit
Muscadet, Pinot gris, some Riesling	Melon
Grenache	Orange Peel
Chablis	Peach
aged oak white, Chardonnay	Pear
some Cabernet Sauvignon	Plums
Beaujolais	Raspberry
some red Bourgogne, Beaujolais	Strawberry
	DRIED FRUITS
some Bordeaux and Burgundy	Cloves
white Burgundy	Chestnut
sweet white wine	Dried fig or pineapple
a few Cabernet	Green Olive
Gewurztanimener	Litchee
old red Bordeaux	Truffle
Beaujolais nouveau (young)	Vanilla
Syrah, Grenache, red Rhone	Black pepper
Bordeaux, Cabernet Sauvignon, Merlot	Green bell pepper
	FLOWERS
Sauvignon blanc	Asparagus
Gewurzt, Riesling	Rose
Cabernet Franc, some Cabernet Sauvignon	Tarragon / Estragon
red Burgundy, Pinot noir	Velvet
some red Bordeaux	Violet
Pinot noir	Peppermint
French old oak	Mint
	VARIOUS
Burgundy	Barnyard / earthy / country

Burgundy, some Beaujolais	Burnt / cooked
some Chardonnay	Butter
some Bordeaux	Cigar box (cedar / tobacco)
very old red wine	Deer
Beaujolais nouveau	Freshness
sweet white wine	Honey
some red Rhone	Meat
Chablis	Mineral
old red Wine	Musk
Bordeaux	Oak
Champagne, white Burgundy	Rising bread
Pouilly Fumé	Smoky
Bordeaux	Tobacco
white Wine, Champagne	Toast

Note that when you "swish" the wine around in the glass, it will settle back to the bottom of the glass, leaving rivulets on the sides – these are called "legs." Good wine has thick legs, poor wine does not.

322 An excuse is worse and more terrible than a lie, for an excuse is a lie guarded

— Pope John Paul II (1920–2005)

When something goes wrong or a mistake is made, you may be asked for an explanation. Explain the reason for the mistake, but do not make an excuse for it. An excuse is just a lie in a different dress. Nobody likes people who make excuses.

323 Try to make the people you work for look good

By making them "look good," we mean helping them to be successful. It could be assisting them in a presentation to a client, in the launch of a product, or in a good report to the company bank manager.

This philosophy should be applied to your immediate supervisor, the president of your organization, or anyone who has a potential say in your career advancement. Remember that everyone likes to look good. If you help them to do so, they will be appreciative. By working to help them achieve their goals, you can expect to share in their success and be rewarded.

324 Be strict in judging yourself and gentle in judging others and you will have no enemies

— Chinese Proverb

In general, it's a good idea to refrain from being critical. Now, this is easier said than done, especially if you are in a position of authority. If you have people reporting to you, it is likely you will have to dole out some form of criticism during the day.

When you do have to be critical, it is important to be sensitive when offering it. Keep the following in mind:

1. Never be critical of, or ask someone not to do, something you are doing yourself. If your office is messy, don't expect them to clean up theirs; if you are dressed poorly, don't ask them to dress better; if you are habitually late, don't tell others to be on time. In order to avoid resentment, you need to hold yourself to a higher standard.

2. When warranted, *ask* others to make changes, don't *tell* them. And frame the request in a positive way that incorporates the group as a whole (if appropriate), rather than individuals personally. Also, make sure you offer a legitimate explanation of why you are asking, e.g., "Your office is the first one visitors see when they arrive, so it would reflect better on the company if you could keep it cleaner," is much better than "Go clean up your office, it's a mess." Or "We encourage everyone to get to choir practice a couple of minutes early to make sure the group starts right on time. We don't have much practice time," is better than "You are often not ready to start when practice begins. Please get here earlier."

The responsibility is for you to effectively communicate any criticism. If you set the proper example, and ask people in a positive way to change their behaviors, you should get the response you need without causing resentment.

...THE TEACHER WILL APPEAR

325 It is important to be honest

Lying is unacceptable. Most of us know this. However, despite this core value there will be times when telling a "white lie" will be necessary in order to avoid hurting other people's feelings. For example, you may have to comment on how cute your friend's baby is when it may not be; or you may have to say how good your date's homemade spaghetti sauce tastes when it doesn't! These types of lies – and only these types – are acceptable as long as they are inconsequential and designed to shelter someone's feelings.

Even though white lies are sometimes acceptable ("sometimes" meaning that you don't make a habit of telling them), understand that there is one type of white lie that is never acceptable. This is when the white lie is "false" flattery. False flattery is when you go out of your way to flatter someone when you know it's not true.

Also known as "sucking up," people will view your actions in a negative way and will, at best, question your motives; at worst they may shun you for it. What is the difference between flattery and sucking up? As a rule of thumb, you should never flatter someone if you would not be prepared say it when they were not around.

Along similar lines, avoid being overly complimentary to your superiors unless it is for a legitimate reason, such as a successful launch of a product, a profitable year, etc. They, along with others, will view your comments for what they are: brown-nosing. And nobody likes a brown-noser.

326 Be flexible about things. Better to bend than to break

— *Scottish proverb*

There will be instances in life when you cannot be flexible. Those times are generally restricted to moral dilemmas. Be firm in both your beliefs and actions.

For most other matters you can afford to be flexible. Be willing to change your position or outlook a little bit if it means keeping harmony at work or at home. A lack of flexibility can lead to relationships (at home and at work) becoming damaged.

327 Trust is like a thin thread. Once you break it, it is almost impossible to put it together again

— Ayub Khan (1907–1974)

Never consciously do anything to breach a trust. It is very, very difficult to correct.

If you are thinking of breaching a trust to help yourself in the short-term – such as telling a secret to endear you to someone – know that the immediate gratification you receive will pale in comparison to the future pain you'll have to endure by having broken that trust. People may say they forgive you, but they will always have doubts about you.

Remember: the future goes on for a long time.

328 Compliments

When you receive a compliment, smile and simply say "thank you" or "thank you, it was nice of you to say that." People extending the compliment want to be appreciated for giving it, but they usually do not want to hear a lengthy response in reply.

329 Don't forget to be kind to strangers. Some who have done this have entertained angels without realizing it

— Hebrews 13:2

One night in the early 1960s, an older African American woman was standing on the side of an Alabama highway trying to endure a lashing rain storm. Her car had broken down and she desperately needed a ride. Soaking wet, she tried to flag down the next car. A young white man stopped to help her, something generally unheard of during the conflict-filled 1960s in the southern U.S. The man took her to safety, helped her get assistance and put her into a taxi. She was in a hurry, but nevertheless took the time to thank him and write down his address. Seven days later a knock came on the man's door. To his surprise, a TV was delivered to his home. A special note was attached. It read: "Thank you so much for assisting me on the highway the other night. The rain drenched not only my clothes but also my spirits. Then you came along. Because of you, I was able to make it to my husband's bedside just before he passed away. God bless you for helping me and unselfishly serving others. Sincerely, Mrs. Nat King Cole" [note: wife of one of America's greatest singers].

— *Author Unknown*

Be friendly to strangers. Not only is it polite, but you may benefit from the contact. You don't know who they are or what their background is. They could turn out to be someone helpful to you and others.

330 Adopt an attitude of gratitude

Begin the week with the attitude that you are thankful – thankful you have a job to go to, a school to attend, or good health. Many people don't have any of those things. If you begin the week in a positive frame of mind, your energy level will be high and your mood light. This will be reflected in your work.

331 Get even with people

But only under one condition: make sure the person you are trying to get even with is someone who has done good to you.

At some point in your life, someone will take advantage of you or hurt you. When this happens, don't be someone who tries to exact revenge on the person who has wronged them. It's a waste of time and energy. Trying to get revenge means they've hurt you twice: the first time when they did their deed to you; and the second time by making you waste time and effort trying to get back at them.

The media is full of stories of spiteful spouses, battling business partners and trash-talking athletes who air their bad feelings and dirty laundry in public. It is unbecoming. Understand that revenge is a waste of time, energy and money, and is a drain on your emotional reserves.

Therefore, if you feel compelled to get even with someone – go ahead. But only get even with the people who have done good to you.

332 Leaders make decisions

Inevitably, not all decisions turn out to be good ones – some turn out to be bad for any number of valid reasons. It could have been that they were based on incorrect information; or they could have been made without having enough information. Regardless of the outcome, a bad decision is generally better than no decision at all. Experience will help with this.

People want direction; they expect their leaders to be decisive and will show respect to those who lead the way. In fact, if a leader does not give his or her subordinates direction, respect will be lost. The challenge, of course, is to ensure that more good decisions are made than bad.

333 Getting information out of people

If you need to get information from someone who is reluctant to say anything, start by getting the person to talk about what is interesting or important to them. By doing so, you create conversational momentum. During the course of the conversation, they will likely become more receptive to you because your actions make it seem as if you are interested in them. After listening and showing interest, attempt to work in your request. They may be more forthcoming at that point.

...ANOTHER IS GIVEN

334 Your most important investment

From a financial perspective, the most important investment you will make in your lifetime will be your marriage.

It is very important to take your time when deciding to marry. Make sure your decision is not based solely on the feelings of infatuation that occur at the beginning of every romantic relationship. Understand that those feelings will become muted over time.

Researchers at Pavia University in Italy have found that the powerful emotions associated with new love are triggered by a molecule they have called the "nerve growth factor" (NGF). The Italian scientists found much higher levels of NGF in the blood of people who had recently fallen in love than in single people and those in long-term relationships. What they also found was that, after one year together, the quantity of NGF – dubbed the "love molecule" – in their blood had fallen to the same level as that of the other groups.[18]

A deep love for each other must serve as the foundation of the marriage. Equally important is that the two of you should share the same core values toward things such as child-rearing, money management and personal integrity. Finally, make sure you can communicate with one another.

A 2005 study by researchers at Ohio State University found that people who get divorced lose on average three-quarters of their personal net worth.[19] Divorce has serious implications on your wealth, not to mention your mental health.

Because you want your marriage to last a lifetime, take the time to ensure all the necessary pieces are in place to build a strong foundation. Don't rush into it.

335 Starting a conversation

SATURDAY

If you need to start a conversation or if you need to make the conversation you are in more interesting, remember the **A, E, I, O, U**s of good conversation:

Association: Find something in common with the other person;

Elevate their mood: Try to make them laugh or make them feel better than before the two of you began the conversation;

Interest: Show actual interest in what they are saying;

Open: Ask **o**pen-ended questions and have **o**pen body language (facing the person, slightly leaning in); and

Try not to talk about yo**u**: Talk about topics other than yourself.

336 He who is without sin among you, let him be the first to throw a stone

SUNDAY

— John 8:7

Do not be quick to condemn others for their actions.

The only time it is acceptable to be judgmental is when it is part of your job – such as when you are a police officer, judge, prosecutor, etc. All of us have things we've done in the past of which we are not very proud. Avoid being vocal and judgmental about other people's actions, because your actions, known or unknown, may be just as bad when seen through others' eyes.

337 Jumping at several small opportunities may get us there more quickly than waiting for one big one to come along

MONDAY

— Sir Hugh Allen (1869–1946)

When presented with an opportunity, go after it regardless of how small it may seem. Any opportunity can lead to positive results. Don't wait around for the perfect opportunity to come along as it may never arrive.

338 Your biggest problem is your biggest problem

— Pierre Lebel (b. 1949)

Never trivialize someone else's problem no matter how small or inconsequential you may think it is.

From their perspective, their problem is serious regardless of how others perceive it. You should be sympathetic.

339 The Turkey

Down on the farm, a wild turkey was chatting with a bull. "I would love to be able to get to the top of that tree so I can have the best view on the farm," sighed the turkey, "but I can't fly."

"Well," said the bull, "why don't you take my manure droppings, make them into a big pile and then climb to the top of the pile so you can reach the bottom branch. From there, you can climb up the other branches and get to the top of the tree."

The turkey did just that and climbed to the top. However, once there, it was not long before the turkey was spotted by a farmer who immediately shot it out of the tree.

The moral of the story is this: bulls**t might help get you to the top, but it won't keep you there.

— Author Unknown

Whoever came up with this story must have envisioned a pretty low tree, because b.s. doesn't get you anywhere in the real world for very long. Most people are able to see through lies and fabrications pretty quickly. Because of that, try to become known for your ability to deliver results rather than for your ability to talk a good game.

When it comes to getting things done, keep in mind what Donald Trump's father used to tell him: "Get in, get it done, get it done right, and get out."

340 A faithful friend is a strong defense; and he that has found such a one has found a treasure

— Apocrypha (Ecclesiasticus 6:14)

If you can find two or three good friends in life – people who will support you under any circumstances – then you will be a very lucky person. The world can be a competitive, cutthroat place that presents daily challenges. Having good friends along to share the journey gives you a foundation of support.

341 Always display good manners, no matter the audience or situation

Good manners demonstrate thoughtfulness, respect and a good up-bringing. Good manners will be appreciated by your boss, your professor and your friends.

They will also help you with that rude colleague or bothersome tele-marketer. It is very difficult to argue with good manners, so if you have to blow somebody off, use them. Your pleasantness will be disarming and will help extricate you from awkward or difficult situations.

342 There are a couple of things to keep in mind when eating soup

Fill your spoon about three-quarters full by putting it in the middle of the bowl. Scoop up the soup by moving the spoon to the far edge of the bowl (roughly the 12 o'clock position). Bring the spoon to your mouth and sip it from the side with as little slurping noise as possible. Do not put the whole spoon in your mouth. When you get to the bottom of the bowl, it is okay to tip the bowl away from you so that you can get at the last of the soup, but don't do it more than twice. As well, make sure that when you lower your spoon into your soup you do it gently, so that it doesn't bang the bottom and make a clanking noise.

343 The world is a book, and those who do not travel read only one page

— Saint Augustine (354–430)

Take every opportunity to travel and see the world when you are young. Traveling the world will give you a broader education than you can get just going to college or university.

344 Fear is never a reason for quitting, it is only an excuse

— Norman Vincent Peale (1898–1993)

Even if you're afraid, don't quit. By seeing a task to its end, you achieve two things: one, the job gets done; and two, you are taught that you can overcome your fears.

345 Body language

According to a study from UCLA, only 7% of a message is communicated verbally (i.e., through words); the remaining 93% is communicated nonverbally: 38% through intonation (how it is said) and 55% through body language.[20]

If this is true, then in order to communicate effectively you need to use your whole body.

When you give any kind of speech or presentation, understand that the audience will quickly form their opinion of you by looking at your posture, and by observing how you use your arms and hands, whether you make eye contact, and your different facial expressions.

Remember that actions speak louder than words. Therefore, it is good to be active when talking to a group or an audience, regardless of its size.

Here are some reasons why actions are important:

1. **Actions make the message more meaningful and memorable**:
   a) people get bored with things that don't move;
   b) people find it hard to resist the temptation to look at moving objects; and
   c) people remember better if they use multiple senses; they remember more of what they see than what they hear.

2. **Actions add "punctuation" to your speech**. In writing there are commas, periods, and exclamation points. You can use your body to punctuate important parts of your speech by stopping, pausing, raising your arm, etc.

Actions also help relieve nervous tension. Most people are nervous when they speak to an audience. That's okay; it's healthy to be nervous because it means you want to do a good job and that the presentation is important to you. You can help relieve this tension by moving around. Harness the nervous energy and make it work for you by using effective actions, rather than letting the nerves work against you.

346 Take every opportunity to expand your career network

WEDNESDAY

Attend as many functions as you can, because they provide a chance to meet new people. Always be willing to approach people you don't know and introduce yourself. If for some reason you can't approach people (too nervous, broken leg), try to make yourself look as approachable as possible to others. You want to encourage others to come to you and introduce themselves. By being approachable, you improve your chances of meeting new people.

In their book *First Impressions: What You Don't Know About How Others See You*,[21] Ann Demarais and Valerie White discuss some things that help make you look approachable:

1. **Body Language**: Smile and have an open posture. Avoid standing in a corner and don't stand with your arms crossed.

2. **Reduce the risk**: People don't want to approach someone when there is the chance of being rejected, so make yourself look as friendly and open as possible.

3. **Fit in**: Try not to stand alone; if you are by yourself, work to move close to a group so that you are on the periphery. Be aware of the dress code and try to make sure that you are neither underdressed nor overdressed.

4. **Look good**: Show that you take care of yourself; this means good grooming and a confident posture.

347 Gossip

THURSDAY

Gossip, which one dictionary defines as "rumor or talk of a personal, sensational or intimate nature," should be avoided at all times.

People generally don't like to learn they have been the subject of gossip. If you feel compelled to talk about someone who is not present, restrict your comments to positive ones. If in doubt about whether something is appropriate or not, Dr. Alan Redpath (1907–1989) said that you need to **THINK**.

Ask yourself the following questions:

T—Is it True?
H—Is it Helpful?
I—Is it Inspiring?
N—Is it Necessary?
K—Is it Kind?

If what you are about to say does not pass all those tests, don't say anything.

348 Attitude

Dr. Charles Swindoll (b. 1934) describes the importance of attitude this way:

"The longer I live, the more I realize the impact of attitude on life. Attitude, to me, is more important than facts. It is more important than the past, than education, than money, than circumstances, than failures, than successes, than what other people think, say, or do. It is more important than appearance, giftedness, or skill. It will make or break a company, a church, a home. The remarkable thing is we have a choice every day regarding the attitude we will embrace for that day.

"We cannot change our past. We cannot change the fact that people will act in a certain way. We cannot change the inevitable. The only thing we can do is play on the one string we have, and that is our attitude. I am convinced that life is 10% what happens to me and 90% how I react to it. And so it is with you. We are in charge of our attitudes."[22]

349 Practice your introduction

Before you attend a social gathering at which you are likely to meet new people, practice your introduction.

Your introduction should include your name (obviously) and something about yourself that establishes what you have in common with the other people at the event. Be energetic and short with your introduction, and be sure to speak clearly and look people in the eye. Your goal should be to give the person a pleasant experience when they meet you and to leave them wanting to talk to you again.

350 I can do all things through Him who strengthens me

— *Philippians 4:13*

Whether your self-confidence arises from your education, your experience, your work ethic or your faith, know that you have the strength to do whatever you set out to do. If ever in doubt about it, just remember where that strength came from.

351 If you are going through hell, keep going

— *Sir Winston Churchill (1874–1965)*

When times are tough, keep plugging ahead. It is important to keep moving – if you stop, you might get stuck. The laws of physics tell us that it is easier to get something going faster when it is already moving than it is to get it started from a stationary position.

If you are going through a tough time, keep going… you'll get to the end faster.

352 Volunteer to fast track your career

When you are building your career, volunteer for committees or associations that get you close to the senior people in your organization. Do this even if the job appears to be menial or trivial. The goal is to become known to the senior people, and the closer you can get to them in a "team" setting, the more they will notice you. The more exposure you can get, the better.

353 If we take people as we find them, we make them worse; but if we treat them as though they are what they should be, we help them to become what they are capable of becoming

— *J.W. von Goethe (1749–1832)*

One of the primary jobs of a leader is to develop the people who report to them. One way to do this is to treat people as if they have already evolved into what you want them to be. If you think your management trainee can someday run the company, treat her as if she is doing it now. She will appreciate the respect and the confidence you show in her, and this will be mirrored in how she responds to you. View people as if they were already at the top of whatever pyramid they aspire to climb – professor, teammate, salesperson. Your confidence in them will be reflected in their performance.

354 There are five parts to successful weight management

1. A regular, sweat-producing exercise program;
2. A well-balanced diet (that includes fruits and vegetables as snacks);
3. Lots of water;
4. Limited intake of caffeine, alcohol, sugar and chemical ingredients; and
5. Sufficient sleep.

355 The best way to learn

Arguably the best way to learn is through experience. It's said that experience is the greatest teacher. As evidence, think of the difference between learning about Paris sitting at your desk in school versus actually walking the streets of that great city. Or consider the teaching effect of actually touching a hot stove burner as opposed to simply being told not to. Try to experience as much of life as you can – the positive parts, that is.

How do you know if a potential experience is going to be positive? Well, if it could cause physical harm to yourself or others, or negatively affect your long-term goals in life, it is probably not going to classify as "positive." Avoid it. Things such as experimenting with drugs, or getting behind the wheel of a car when you've been drinking, or having an extramarital affair – are all experiences you can do without. Nothing good comes from these types of experiences. Embrace the good ones; reject the bad ones.

356 Be a smile starter

Most smiles start with another smile. Try it. Walk into a room with a nice smile on your face and watch for the response. People will notice and give you one right back.

When you want to introduce yourself to someone new, walk up to them with a smile on your face. They will inevitably smile back, and your contact – as brief as it may be – will be off to a good start.

357 Who is a wise man?
He who studies all the time.
Who is strong?
He who can control himself.
Who is rich?
He who is happy with what he has

> — *The Talmud*

358 Be not afraid of growing slowly,
be afraid of only standing still

> — *Chinese proverb*

Do not be disappointed if your progress seems slow. Some things take time. The only time you should be worried is if you're not progressing because you're not trying hard enough.

359 Leadership is action, not position

TUESDAY

Just because you are named the team captain or made the president of your company, it does not make you a leader (although you probably showed some skill to get there in the first place). Once you are at the top, don't think you will automatically command respect as a leader. If you think that way, you probably won't be in charge for very long. It's your actions once you are there that keep you a leader, not the title.

360 Don't hire family

WEDNESDAY

When running a business, try to avoid hiring family members of existing employees. This is because you may be faced with having to let that person go. The original employee will very likely be upset with you, and two things may happen: that person's attitude and performance could deteriorate because they are upset; or they may quit in support of their family member. It's just a good situation to avoid.

361 The greatest mathematical discovery of all time

THURSDAY

Albert Einstein (1879–1955), when asked what he thought was the most powerful force in the universe, responded that it was "compound interest." Compound interest is the interest earned on both the original investment and the accumulated interest.

In fact, he jokingly called the compound interest "Rule of 72" the greatest mathematical discovery of all time.

The Rule of 72 gives you a quick way of determining how good or bad a potential investment is. The rule says that, in order to find the number of years required to double your money at a given interest rate, you can divide the projected rate of return (or the interest rate) into 72. For example, if you want to know how long it will take to double your money at 8% interest, divide 8 into 72 and you get nine years. The rule works for all interest rates less than 20%.

...NOT PERFECTION

The rule also works backwards. Say you want to double your money in six years: divide six into 72 and you will find it will require a compound interest rate of about 12%.

This rule helps explain another popular investment adage: the "7/11" rule. This guideline says that if you can get a 7% compound annual return, your investment will double about every 11 years; if you can get an 11% compound annual return, your investment will double every seven years.

The basic lesson here is the importance of time and how compounding works.

The more time you have, the greater the compounding effect. Accordingly, start saving as soon as you can. This way, your money works for you rather than you working for your money. The earlier you start, the harder your money will work for you.

Finally, one cautionary note with respect to investment returns. If someone tries to tell you that you can consistently get a compound annual rate of return of anything more than say 17.5% (or about 7% above historical stock market returns), run. At the very least, be wary. Rates of return like that are not sustainable. Your investment could be in jeopardy.

362 The House of 1,000 Mirrors

Long ago, in a small, faraway village, there was a place known as the House of 1,000 Mirrors. A small, happy little dog learned of this place and decided to visit. When he arrived, he bounced happily up the stairs to the doorway of the house. He looked through the doorway with his ears lifted high and his tail wagging as fast as it could. To his great surprise, he found himself staring at 1,000 other happy little dogs with their tails wagging just as fast as his. He smiled a great smile, and was answered with 1,000 great smiles just as warm and friendly. As he left the house, he thought to himself, "This is a wonderful place. I will come back and visit it often."

In this same village, another little dog, who was not quite as happy as the first one, heard about the house and decided to visit. When he got there, he slowly climbed the stairs and hung his head low as he looked into the door. When he looked in, he saw 1,000 unfriendly looking dogs staring back at him. He growled at them and was horrified to see 1,000 little dogs growling back at him. He thought to himself, "This is a horrible place, and I will never come back again." And he left.

— *Japanese folktale*

Learn from this story that every face you see is a mirror. What kind of reflection do you see in the faces of the people you meet?

363 One of the more challenging meals to eat is lobster

SATURDAY

Eating lobster is the only time in your adult life when wearing a bib is acceptable.

There are four steps involved in eating lobster:

Step 1: Twist off the claws with your hands and break the tips with the nutcracker (which should be supplied; if not, ask for one). It is okay to use your fingers to remove the meat; however, a more polite way is to use the lobster fork – a short, thin, two-pronged fork.

Step 2: Twist and separate the tail from the body and use the lobster fork to dig out the tail meat; you can also use your fingers to do this.

Step 3: Remove any green paste (called the tomalley) by scraping it off with your fork.

Step 4: Twist off the lobster's smaller claws and use your teeth to squeeze out the meat. Your lobster fork may also be of help getting into the claws.

Be sure to have a napkin handy to wipe off your fingers when you are done. And don't forget to use the finger bowl… don't mistake it for lemon soup.

SUCCESS

364

SUNDAY

It is the quality of our work which will please God and not the quantity

— Mahatma Gandhi (1869–1948)

Make sure you do the best job you can possibly do, no matter what the task.

Many people take on extra work in the hope that doing so will help to advance their careers. This attitude is commendable; however, be sure to take on only as much extra work as you can effectively handle. It is better to be known for doing excellent work than to be thought of as someone who does a lot of work but not very well.

365

MONDAY

The time to repair the roof is when the sun is shining

— John F. Kennedy (1917–1963)

Don't procrastinate. If you have a job to do, get started on it. It is easier to get it done when you have ample time and are not under pressure. Leaving things until the last minute often leads to rushed projects and shoddy workmanship. Start projects as soon as you can to allow yourself time to do a good job.

FINAL NOTE:

The lessons listed above are only some of the hundreds – maybe thousands – of life lessons that are helpful for a high school graduate to know. You will no doubt come across many quotes or stories that have meaning for you and would be helpful for you to remember. We encourage you to write them down here.

...TO FOLLOW THROUGH

REFERENCES

1. Salovey, P. & Mayer, J.D. (1990). "Emotional Intelligence". *Imagination, Cognition, and Personality* 9, 185–211.

2. There is a very good book by Susan RoAne called *How To Work A Room* [Warner Books, 1988] in which she offers many hints on effectively working a room.

3. Evans, C., Chalmers, J., Capewell, S., Redpath, A., Finalyson, A., Boyd, J., et al. (2000). "I Don't Like Mondays". *British Medical Journal* 320:218–219.

4. Malouf, Doug (1988). *How to Create and Deliver a Dynamic Presentation*, p. 81. American Society for Training.

5. Wharton Applied Research Center, Wharton School, University of Pennsylvania (1981). *A study of the effects of the use of overhead transparencies on business meetings.*

6. Jordan-Evans, Sharon and Beverly Kaye (2002). *Love 'Em or Lose 'Em: Getting Good People to Stay. 2nd Edition.* Berrett-Koehler Publishers.

7. Please see www.greatplacetowork.com.

8. Chilton, David (1993). *The Wealthy Barber.* Stoddart Publishing.

9. National Survey of Family Growth Data (2002). Guttmacher Institute.

10. YouGov PLC study (2005). Commissioned by The Confident Club and Promothean AV.

11. Slavin, R. (1994). *Educational Psychology, Theory and Practice.* Allyn and Bacon.

12. Lytle, C.D. et al. (1992). "Filtration Sizes of Human Immunodeficiency Virus Type 1 and Surrogate Viruses Used to Test Barrier Materials". *Applied and Environmental Microbiology,* vol. 58–2.

13. Weller, S. (1993). "A Meta-Analysis of Condom Effectiveness in Reducing Sexually Transmitted HIV". *Social Science and Medicine* 36:12, 1635–1644.

14. Carey, Ronald F., et al. (1992). "Effectiveness of Latex Condoms as a Barrier to Human Immunodeficiency Virus-sized Particles Under Conditions of Simulated Use". *Sexually Transmitted Diseases* 19:4, 230–234.

15. Kettering, Jim (June 1993). "Efficacy of Thermoplastic Elastometers and Latex Condoms as Viral Barriers". *Contraception* vol. 47, 563–564.

16. Jones, Elise F. and Forrest, J.D. (1992). "Contraceptive Failure Rates Based on the 1988 National Survey of Family Growth". *Family Planning Perspectives* 24:1, 12 and 18. *See also* Gordon, R. (1989). *Journal of Sex and Marital Therapy* vol. 15, 5–30.

17. Please see www.terroir-france.com.

18. Emanuele, E., Politi, P., Bianchi, M., Minoretti, P., Bertona, M., Geroldi, D., Interdepartmental Center for Research in Molecular Medicine (CIRMC), University of Pavia (November 2005). "Raised Plasma Nerve Growth Factor Levels Associated With Early-stage Romantic Love". *Psychoneuroendocrinology.*

19. Zagorsky, J., Center for Human Resource Research, Ohio State University (2005). "Marriage and Divorce's Impact on Wealth". *Journal of Sociology* vol. 41:4, 406–424.

20. Mehrabian, A. (1968). "Communication Without Words". *Psychology Today* 2, 53–55.

21. Demarais, A. and White, V. (2004). *First Impressions: What You Don't Know About How Others See You.* Bantam Books.

22. A similar quote first appeared on pages 206–207 of Dr. Swindoll's book *Strengthening Your Grip* [1982, Word Books]. More great quotes from Dr. Swindoll can be found at www.insight.org.

INSPIRATIONAL SAYINGS
DISPLAYED THROUGHOUT THE BOOK

1. When you get right down to the root meaning of *succeed*, you find that it simply means to follow through. — F.W. Nichol

2. When the student is ready, the teacher appears. — Zen Buddhist proverb

3. When we lose one blessing, another is often given in its place. — C.S. Lewis

4. There is no one luckier than he who thinks himself so. — German proverb

5. Love is the triumph of imagination over intelligence. — H. L. Mencken

6. Strive for excellence, not perfection. — H. Jackson Brown Jr.

7. The weak can never forgive. Forgiveness is the attribute of the strong. — Mahatma Gandhi

8. To live a creative life, we must lose our fear of being wrong. — Joseph Chilton Pearce

9. Respect yourself and others will respect you. — Confucius

10. Always laugh when you can. It is cheap medicine. — Lord Byron

11. Trust yourself, you know more than you think you do. — Benjamin Spock

12. Laughter is the shortest distance between two people. — Victor Borge

13. Life itself is the most wonderful fairytale of all. — Hans Christian Andersen

INDEX

ABOUT THE AUTHORS

JIM PRATT

Immediately after Jim graduated with a business degree from the University of Alberta in 1984, he and Jane moved to Europe, where Jim played professional basketball. Returning to Canada, Jim obtained an MBA from the Richard Ivey School of Business at the University of Western Ontario, moving on to work on Bay Street as an investment banker and becoming vice president for a large national investment dealer. In 1992, they left the security of a steady paycheck to invest in a small food manufacturing company in B.C. The company has since been named one of Canada's Best Managed Companies and been listed as one of Canada's 100 fastest-growing companies a total of four times. In 1997 Jim was named one of B.C.'s *Top 40 under 40* business achievers.

JANE PRATT

A former Miss Teen Edmonton and first runner-up Miss Teen Canada, Jane married her high school sweetheart and was a fitness instructor, travel industry professional and model before becoming a stay-at-home mom to their three children. Over the years, she has served as president of a chapter of Beta Sigma Phi, a philanthropic women's organization; acted as president of a local chapter of Canadian Parents for French, an organization dedicated to promoting French language in Canadian schools; and been involved in numerous parent–teacher organizations. She has been voted 'World's Best Mom' on a number of occasions by each of her three children.

Please visit www.turtleonafencepost.ca for more information.

CPSIA information can be obtained at www.ICGtesting.com
Printed in the USA
LVOW120126160413

329266LV00001B/2/P